THREE MUSICALS

BY

JAN CALLNER AND BILL WHEELER

FROM THE SERIES

"ALMOST - EVERYONE SHOWS"

OUR VISION:

CHILDREN, PRETEENS, TEENS, ADULTS, AMATEURS, AND PROFESSIONALS CAN ALL PERFORM THESE CHARMING, WELL-CRAFTED THEATER PIECES. PERFECT FOR: FAMILY THEATER, SCHOOL PRODUCTIONS, CAMPS, THEATERS FOR YOUNG AUDIENCES, AND MORE.

ALMOST - EVERYONE SHOWS

A CREATIVE JOURNEY

FROM

MIKE AND ME PRODUCTIONS

Three One-Act Musicals "Almost - Everyone Shows"

The Frog Prince, The Magic Fish, Fee, Fie, Foe, Fum...Jack's Tale

Copyright © 2025
Jan Callner

All rights reserved. This book or any portion thereof may be used for amateur, school, camp, and related productions royalty-free. Teachers, counselors, etc. may reproduce pages as needed.

Professional and/or commercial productions require permission from the copyright holder/publisher Mike and Me Productions: info@jancallner.com.
Excerpts may not be reproduced or used in any other manner other than those described above without the express written permission of the publisher except for the use of brief quotations in a book review.

Mike and Me Productions
www.jancallner.com
ISBN 978-0-9862720-4-2

ACKNOWLEDGEMENTS

THIS COLLECTION IS DEDICTED TO WILLIAM (BILL) WAYNE WHEELER

1953-2006

Bill was one of the funniest and most talented people I have ever known. We worked together for twenty-eight years. I miss him daily.

THANKS TO

CHRISTINE BOYKA KLUGE for her extraordinary ARTWORK

MICHAEL CALDERWOOD for his TECHNICAL AND CREATIVE SKILLS

ALL THE PERFORMERS THROUGH THE YEARS WHO HAVE SHARED THEIR TALENT

JAN CALLNER is a multi-talented playwright/composer/lyricist/singer/actress/director/pianist/teacher and lover of theater. She believes in the power of the stage. The power to bring the world in all its glory and failure to life right before our eyes.

BILL WHEELER was a performer, director, writer, and teacher whose life was the theater. He worked in New York City for years and passed in Key West, Florida where he was active with the Waterfront Playhouse.

NOTE FROM THE CREATOR: JAN CALLNER

These three titles are a labor of love—and only a fraction of the musicals for young audiences my partners and I have created. Technology and I have evolved to the point where I can finally release them in a usable form for the public to enjoy. (Granted, technology evolved much faster than I did.)

The titles in this collection are retellings of much-loved children's stories—two Brothers Grimm and one old English. Yet, they are fresh and modern with timeless songs and snappy dialogue.

THE FROG PRINCE was written in 1996 for Westco Productions, a company based in Westchester County, New York. Thousands of children arrived at a theater in White Plains, New York, for a week-long run of nine shows. Then, the show went on tour to children's hospitals and other facilities for people with disabilities. Since then, productions have been mounted on both the East and West Coasts. I've included some drawings by our young audiences.

A full-length recording of the play and music featuring Broadway actors received the Early Childhood News Directors' Choice Award and was featured annually on RADIO ACTIVE KIDS. Producer Sagan Thacker called it his favorite show "ever." I play the wacky Fairy Godmother, James Gerth the narrator frog, Aloysius, Michael Farina is the Prince, Deborah Spahr, the selfish Princess, John Fava plays the King, and Joan Thunhorst the Queen. The recording is available on all streaming platforms.

THE MAGIC FISH is even older—its genesis a regional theater in upstate New York. Bill Wheeler and I collaborated on the story of "The Fisherman and His Wife" to establish a theater-for-young-audiences tradition that we pursued for thirty years. This show has had many productions, including at Wings Theater in NYC's Greenwich Village. We recorded this show too. Bill played the friendly Pel-I-Can, James Gerth the Magic Fish, John Treacy Egan played the Fisherman, and Vaneese Thomas the Wife. The songs in this show are some of my favorites, like "Just One Wish" and "Good Husband."

Hold on for *FEE, FIE, FOE, FUM... JACK'S TALE*. If I had to pick a favorite, it might be this one. It just tickles my particular funny bone. Bill wrote most of this script, and I think it's some of his best work. My favorite song in this production is "Jack Come Back." And I am in love with the doofy Giant. We're working on a recording, but as of this release, none is available. I'll have reference music available on my website for those who purchase this compilation: www.jancallner.com

These shows are TIMELESS. They speak to who we are as human beings (and, yes, anthropomorphized frogs, fish, and pelicans). Without theater, we interpret the world through a single pair of eyes. With theater, we are gifted with a hundred pairs.

TABLE OF CONTENTS

THE FROG PRINCE

Script	1
Music	36

THE MAGIC FISH

Script	71
Music	103

FEE, FIE, FOE, FUM....JACK'S TALE

Script	152
Music	181

THE FROG PRINCE

A ONE-ACT
MUSICAL FOR CHILDREN

Cover art Christine Boyka Kluge

Script, Music, Lyrics
By
Jan Callner

Copyright 1995, 2014, 2025
Jan Callner
mike and me productions

CHARACTERS

ALOYSIUS/ALICIA	The narrator as well as a character in the play.
THE FROG PRINCE	The Prince who becomes a frog and then becomes human again. A victim of circumstance, an innocent.
THE PRINCESS	A spoiled brat who has a change of heart
KING	Her Father. Not terribly noble or firm, but a King, nonetheless.
QUEEN	Sweet loving mother, a little ditsy
FAIRYGODMOTHER	Conniving, but not evil
OPTIONAL CHORUS	A chorus of frogs to be featured in "Lily Pad Heaven," "The Golden Ball," "Friends," and "Sometimes A Promise."

SCENES

SCENE 1	The Princess's garden
SCENE 2	Same garden eighteen years later
SCENE 3	The Palace
SCENE 4	The Princess's bedroom
SCENE 5	The Garden

SONGS

1. LILY PAD HEAVEN PRELUDE Aloysius/Alicia
2. THE MAD SONG   Fairy godmother
3. LILY PAD HEAVEN   Aloysius/Alicia and Frog Prince
4. ANOTHER NIGHT AT THE PALACE   King, Queen, Princess
5. ROYAL FANFARE   Instrumental
6. EENY MEENY   Princess
7. THE GOLDEN BALL   Princess and Aloysius/Alicia
8. FRIENDS   Princess and Prince
9. SOMETIMES A PROMISE   All

SET PIECES AND PROPS

Set Pieces	Props
A clump of trees	A bench for the garden
A wishing well	Two golden balls (volleyball size)
A table – 4 chairs	Two top hats and canes
The Princess's bed	A crone's staff
A large flat pillow	Fire extinguisher for puffs of smoke

(Author's note: foamcore board works great to make shapes needed for trees, the well, tables, etc. For instance, the shape of a fancy table can be adhered in silhouette to a plain portable table.)

COSTUMES

Princess	Scene I: Simple white nightgown, oversized baby bonnet,
	Scene II: Elegant day dress of a Princess
	Scene III: Same dress. Add a crown
	Scene IV: Nightgown over dress
	Scene V: Elegant Princess dress
Frog Prince	Scene I: Baby outfit, bonnet: Change into Frog costume
	Scene II: Frog costume
	Scene III: Frog costume jazzed up a little for court
	Scene IV: Same
	Scene V: Prince costume
Aloysius/Alicia	Scene I-II: Basic Frog costume
	Scene III-V: Add court dress
King and Queen:	Same royal attire throughout
Fairy godmother:	An outlandish attire that suggests magic
Chorus:	Variations on frog costumes

THE FROG PRINCE
by
JAN CALLNER

SCENE 1

A CLUMP OF TREES BIG ENOUGH TO SERVE AS A CHANGING SCREEN. A WISHING WELL. POSSIBLY A BENCH. ALOYSIUS/ALICIA IS ON STAGE.

SONG #1 LILY PAD HEAVEN (short version.)

**THE ROAD TO HEAVEN'S NOT PAVED WITH GOLD.
IT MAY NOT EVEN BE SHINY.
IT DOESN'T MATTER WHAT YOU'VE BEEN TOLD,
SO DON'T GO STUMBLING BLINDLY.**

**YOU NEED TO STEP RIGHT, CROSS LEFT,
TIP YOUR HAT AT A JAUNTY ANGLE.
WALK THIS WAY BUT WATCH YOUR STEP.
YOU DON'T WANNA GET ALL TANGLED.**

**LILY PAD HEAVEN IS THE PLACE I CALL MY HOME!
IT'S ALWAYS THERE, WAITING FOR ME,
NO MATTER WHERE I ROAM.**

**SO IF YOU STEP RIGHT, CROSS LEFT,
DON'T GO STUMBLING BLINDLY.
WALK THIS WAY BUT WATCH YOUR STEP,
YOU'LL BE THANKING ME KINDLY.**

AL: Greetings. That was my theme song. How'd you like it? I call it "Lily Pad Heaven." Get it? "Lily Pad" cause I'm a frog you see. And frogs like lily pads. My name is Aloysius/Alicia. I am just an ordinary frog, although I DO have a lotta class. Now, I know what you're thinking, BUT…I am not THE frog as in THE Frog Prince! But I'm here to tell you his story.

Once upon a time there were two babies. They were from neighboring kingdoms. (The Prince and Princess enter in baby bonnets carrying baby bottles.) Their parents were the best of friends and tried to get them together for playdates as often as possible.

PRINCESS: (Baby talk) Abba dabba babba.

PRINCE: Na ma na manna.

AL: They were very sweet children. One was a prince…

PRINCE: Na manna.

AL: And one was a prin…*cess*!

PRINCESS: Ba babba.

AL: It was hoped by both kingdoms, that one day they would marry and unite these kingdoms into one magnificent kingdom! But for right now, they just wanted to be kids.

(Prince and Princess sing and play "Ring Around the Rosie in baby talk.)

AL: Now…it just so happened that the parents of the Prince forgot to invite someone to his first birthday party. And this someone was pretty important. It was the Prince's fairy godmother! This fairy godmother was usually a pretty nice lady, but she LOVED parties.

FGM: I LOVE PARTIES!

AL: And when she didn't get invited to one, BOY, was she MAD!

FGM: BOY AM I MAD! How could they? How could they? How could they?

    SONG#2 THE MAD SONG

**IT TAKES A LOT TO MAKE ME MAD,
A RUDE REMARK IS NOT SO BAD,
AN INSULT HERE, A COMMENT THERE
DOES NOT SEND ME INTO DEEP DESPAIR!**

**AND WHEN SOMEONE CUTS IN FRONT OF ME
IN LINE TO SEE A MOVIE
DO I SHOUT? WHY NO!
I SIMPLY GO ABOUT MY BUSINESS…BUT**

**A PARTY, A PARTY! NOW THAT'S ANOTHER
MATTER ENTIRELY!
I'M THE DIVA OF THE PARTY SET,**

> **HOW COULD THEY FORGET,**
> **SOME GROSS MISTAKE, A GRAND FAUX PAS,**
> **NOT TO THINK OF ME AT ALL,**
> **NOW THAT MAKES ME MAD!**
> **THERE'S NOTHING I LOVE MORE THAN**
>
> **RIBBONS, BALLOONS, ICE CREAM, AND CAKE.**
> **PARTY FAVORS HOME I CAN TAKE.**
> **GOODY BAGS FILLED TO THE BRIM!**
> **LOTS OF PRIZES I CAN WIN!**
>
> **PERHAPS THERE WILL BE A PIÑATA,**
> **WHERE EVERYONE MIGHT HAVE A CHANCE**
> **TO BLINDFOLD AND GIVE IT A SWATTA**
> **THEN DANCE THE MEXICAN DANCE.**
>
> **BUT!**
> **SO WHAT IF THERE'S A PIÑATA!**
> **WHAT AM I TALKING ABOUT?**
> **YOU SEE, SINCE THEY FORGOTTA,**
> **I'M THE ONE WHO IS LEFT OUT!**
>
> **SOME GROSS MISTAKE, A GRAND FAUX PAS,**
> **NOT TO THINK OF ME AT ALL!**
> **NOW THAT…THAT MAKES ME MAD!**
>
> SO MAD! I'll teach them a lesson! All of them! A lesson they'll never forget! I'll cast a spell on the Prince. That's what I'll do! Now where are those "cute" little babies?

BABIES: Abba Dabba abba?

FGM: Ah! There you are! Now, let's see. How about this? A VIS A VAS A VOO. A SCHNOOK A SCHNACK A SCHNOO. I'LL TURN YOU INTO A KANGAROO! POOF!

Oh my! Much too large a creature. Let me see. I'll try…A FLICK A FLACK A FLOG. A TICK A TACK A TOG. I'LL TURN YOU INTO A LITTLE FROG! POOF! Yes, much better. (She picks up stuffed toy frog from behind the tree and walks DSC with it and sets it down.) That'll show 'em. See you later Froggie!

FP: Ribbit.

SHE EXITS TO MUSICAL TAG

AL:	Do you believe that?! Do you know what she did? She destabilized the entire geopolitical balance of the region! Uh, that is, she turned our Prince into a FROG…not that that's all that bad.
PRINCESS:	(Coming from behind the tree and looking for her friend.) Pwince? Pwince? Where are you? (Seeing the frog) Oh my! Oh Pwince! Pwincey! What did that wacky wady go and do? Where's my Pwince?! PAPA!!!
KING:	(entering) Whatever is the matter, Princess? Why are you crying?
PRINCESS:	A wabba dabba wabba dabba WAAHH! (Of course her father cannot understand her.)
KING:	(Looking around and seeing the frog.) Oh, my! Did this little frog scare you? Now, now, Princess. Don't be afraid. A frog won't hurt you. He's just one of nature's creatures. He belongs on this wonderful planet. And frogs do so much good too! Can you imagine how many flies and mosquitoes there would be if the frogs didn't eat them?
PRINCESS:	GASP!
KING:	That's right. They love to eat those bugs!
PRINCESS:	(Whispering) Fwies! Mosqueetoes. YUCK! Poor Pwincey!
KING:	Come along now, Princess. It's time for lunch. (They exit.)
PRINCESS:	Ba Ba, Pwincey.
FP:	Wibbit! Wibbit!
AL:	This is where I come in. Naturally this kid had never been a frog before, so uh, you know, I had to show him the ropes. Like where the juiciest flies hang out…where the best lily pads are…all the stuff we froggies need to know. (He walks over and picks up toy.) So Pwincey…What say the two of us go for a hop?
FP:	Wibbit!! (OK!)
AL:	That voice! We've got to do something about it. You sound like you have a kid in your throat. Lucky for you I'm bilingual. Work with me here. Clear your throat and repeat after me. (As he walks behind tree with frog. Then, a la Professor Higgins:) "The Road To Heaven's not paved with gold….

HE EMERGES FROM BEHIND THE TREE, HAVING DROPPED THE TOY, EMERGING WITH THE ACTOR PLAYING FP IN HIS FROG COSTUME.

FP: (Clears throat) Wibbee, Wibboo, Wibwib, woo woo wa.

AL: Not bad. Again!

FP: (Growing more confident) Wibbee, Wibboo, Wibwib, woo woo wa.

AL: Yes! One more time!!!

MUSICAL INTRO AS FP REPEATS HIS PHRASE WITH MORE GUSTO

SONG #3: LILY PAD HEAVEN

**THE ROAD TO HEAVEN'S NOT PAVED WITH GOLD.
IT MAY NOT EVEN BE SHINY!
IT DOESN'T MATTER WHAT YOU'VE BEEN TOLD.
SO DON'T GO STUMBLING BLINDLY.**

**YOU NEED TO STEP RIGHT, CROSS LEFT,
TIP YOUR HAT AT A JAUNTY ANGLE.
WALK THIS WAY BUT WATCH YOUR STEP,
YOU DON'T WANNA GET ALL TANGLED. (REPEAT)**

**LILY PAD HEAVEN IS THE PLACE I CALL MY HOME!
IT'S ALWAYS THERE, WAITING FOR ME,
NO MATTER WHERE I ROAM.**

**SO IF YOU STEP RIGHT, CROSS LEFT,
DON'T GO STUMBLING BLINDLY.
WALK THIS WAY, BUT WATCH YOUR STEP
AND YOU'LL BE THANKING ME KINDLY.**

(SPOKEN) TAKE IT FROGGIE!

**FP: WIBBEE WOO WOO, WOO WOO WOO WOO,
WIB WIB (ETC)
WOO, WOO WOO WAH WIB, WOOPS! ETC**

**LILY PAD HEAVEN IS THE PLACE I CALL MY HOME.
IT'S ALWAYS THERE,**

IT'S ALWAYS WAITING FOR ME,
NO MATTER WHERE I ROAM.

SO IF YOU (ETC.)
YOU'LL BE THANKING ME,
YOU'LL BE THANKING ME KINDLY.

AL: Come on kid, let's hop over to my pad and grab some lunch

MUSICAL TAG

SCENE 2: EIGHTEEN YEARS LATER

AL: And so, the years went on…Eighteen years to be exact. Back at the Prince's castle his parents missed him terribly, while in the other kingdom, the Princess was growing up into a…well, into a…well, it's kind of hard to describe what she was growing up into. Let's give a listen, shall we?

PRINCESS: (Entering backwards and shouting rudely offstage. She is carrying a gold ball.) And if I CAN'T go to Tahiti for vacation then I'm just not going back to college! I don't care if I don't get my degree! What do I need a degree for anyway?? I'M A PRINCESS!!!

(To herself). Boy, some people! What do they EXPECT from me? I mean, I have a BUSY schedule! It's hard WORK being a princess. First I have to get UP. Then I have to have people DRESS me. Then someone does my HAIR…another one does my NAILS and all the WHILE I'm TRYING to sip my tea. Then when THAT:S all done it's time for lunch. Then AFTER lunch, the whole thing starts all OVER again. I hardly have ANY spare time for relaxation! Why TODAY I could BARELY steal away for five minutes to play with my VERY special gold ball. (She throws it up in the air.) Ooooo. It's so beautiful…Just like me.

FP: (Who has been sitting motionless on the well.) Ribbitt. (Hello.)

PRINCESS: What was that?

FP: Ribbitt, Ribbitt. (Want a fly?)

PRINCESS: (Sees Frog) Eeew! Ribbitt yourself. What is a toad like you doing in my own private relaxation garden?

FP: Ribbitt. Eating lunch. And I'm not a toad. I'm a frog.

PRINCESS: Whatever. Lunch?

FP: Yes! Best flies in the kingdom. Right here!

PRINCESS: (Sardonically) Wouldn't you know it.

FP: Say, I heard you talking to yourself.

PRINCESS: What were you doing eavesdropping on my own private conversation?

FP: Well, I guess I was probably eavesdropping!

PRINCESS: The very idea! I could have your head for that you know!

FP: And what would you do with it?

PRINCESS: With what?

FP: My head. What would you do with it?

PRINCESS: Oh, I don't know! Forget it!

FP: Forgotten! Wanna play catch?

PRINCESS: With a frog?

FP: No, Actually, with the ball.

PRINCESS: I don't think I want a frog touching my beautiful golden ball.

FP: And why is that?

PRINCESS: You might get frog stuff on it. And anyway, I might muss my hair.

FP: Your hair looks a little mussed already.

PRINCESS: (Truly alarmed.) It does? Where???

FP: Well, I don't have a mirror, but…

PRINCESS: (Frantically) A mirror, a mirror…I need a mirror! Oh maybe I can see my reflection in the water in the well. (She leans over to look in the well.) Oh, NO!

SFX DROP AND SPLASH
My beautiful golden ball!!!

FP: I guess you can't see yourself in the water now with that big gold ball floating down there.

PRINCESS: You nincompoop! That's not the issue!!!

FP: Issue? Nincompoop? Why are you calling me a nincompoop? And is that bad?

PRINCESS; I can do anything I want! Have you forgotten? I AM A PRINCESS!!

FP: Oh, you know, I did forget for a second. Well, if you can do anything, then I suppose you can get your ball out of the well.

PRINCESS: Well, of course I…can't. How can I do that? I'm not a (realizing what she's about to say and suddenly becoming sweet.) frog. Oh, froggie dear, I'm so sorry I called you a nincompoop.

FP: Oh, that's all right. (To audience) I guess it WAS bad!

PRINCESS: How far down in that well do you think my ball is?

FP: Hmmmm. I'd say a good twenty feet.

PRINCESS: I just don't know what kind of strong, capable, athletic creature could possibly descend into a well and carry up a golden ball twenty feet. Why it's nigh impossible!

FP: Nigh impossible, eh?

PRINCESS: Well, yes, except for the most agile of creatures.

FP: (Checking himself out) Hmmm, strong, capable, athletic, agile…Yep. I could probably do it.

PRINCESS: Oh, would you? Could you?

FP: I think I would, I think I could…If you would give ME something…

PRINCESS: Oh, diamonds, rubies, gold; whatever you want Froggie dear.

FP:	What would I do with diamonds or rubies, or gold? I'm a frog. I don't want any of those!
PRINCESS:	Well, then, what DO you want?
FP:	Just something simple.
PRINCESS:	(Under her breath.) Good. (Aloud) Then tell me.
FP:	I want to share dinner with you.
PRINCESS:	DINNER? EWWWW!
FP:	Yes, dinner. And then…
PRINCESS:	You mean there's more?
FP:	Yes, then I would like to sleep on your silk pillow. You DO have silk pillows, don't you?
PRINCESS;	Of course I have silk pillows you, you Nin…FROG. But YOU'LL not be sleeping on one! NO DEAL!
FP:	Very well, I'll be leaving you then. (He starts to go.)
PRINCESS:	Oh drat! (To herself.) Wait a minute. If I promise him that he can dine with me and that he can sleep on a silk pillow, he'll get my ball…And then after I have my ball back safe and sound, I'll just tell him I've changed my mind…and that will be that! Wait, Froggie!
FP:	Yes, Princess?
PRINCESS:	I've decided to let you dine with me…and to let you sleep on my silk pillow.
FP:	Oh, rapture, Oh joy…
PRINCESS:	Oh, please.
FP:	Oh, goody, goody. I'll just put on my trusty goggles and my special T-shirt with the large letter F on the front and my froggie flippers, oh, never mind, I don't need those. One should always

	have the proper equipment for the job, ya know…doot da doot da doot…All right! Here I go!

SFX. DROP AND SPLASH SOUND AGAIN

PRINCESS:	Oh goody! I knew I'd get my way.
AL:	(Entering) Hold it right there!
PRINCESS:	Oh, no! Not another frog!
AL:	Oh, yes. Another frog.
FP:	(From the well) Glub, glub, glub. (He sings) "Sailing, Sailing, over the bounding main."
AL:	Only I'm not as gullible as my friend down there!
PRINCESS:	Why, whatever do you mean, Mr., Mr.…?
AL:	Mr./Ms. Aloysius/Alicia T. Frog to you Miss.
PRINCESS;	And "Princess" to you, sir/ma'am.
FP:	Glub, Glub, blub. "Sailing, Sailing, over the bounding main."
PRINCESS:	This is a bad dream.
AL:	It is NOT a dream, Princess. And I'm here to tell you that I know what you're up to.
PRINCESS:	And what is that, Mr./Ms. Frog?
AL:	You made a promise to my friend and you don't mean to keep it.
PRINCESS:	Oh, pooh! What does it matter? He's just a frog! A promise to a FROG doesn't mean anything! It's not like a real promise! Anyway, I can do anything I like! I am a Prin-CESS!
FP:	(From the well) I'VE GOT IT, I'VE GOT IT! One more foot and I'll be at the top!
Princess:	(Rushing over to the well with Al.) Come on Froggie, I knew you could do it. I knew you could. You're the best! Come on! A few more inches! You can do it! (The ball appears at the top. She grabs it.) Hooray! I've got it! So long, Mr. Toad!

SHE EXITS. SFX SAME AS BEFORE. THE FP FALLS BACK DOWN INTO THE WELL.

FP: Glub, Glub, HELP, glub. "Sailing, sailing…Oh brother!

AL: Hey kid, you all right?

FP: Is that you, Al?

AL: It's me all right. Come on, I'll help you out.

SCENE CHANGE MUSIC: LILY PAD HEAVEN

SCENE 3 **The palace**.

THE TABLE IS SET FOR DINNER. THE KING AND QUEEN ARE WAITING FOR THEIR DAUGHTER. SHE IS ALSO ONSTAGE BUT IN ANOTHER LIGHT TO INDICATE HER ROOM. SHE IS GETTING READY, AS USUAL.

AL: Say kids, while our friend the Frog Prince is drying out at my pad, what say we peek in at the palace later that very evening.

MUSICAL GLISS

Hmmmm. Very nice. Oh, yes, lovely. I see the King and Queen in the dining hall. They appear to be…they appear to be waiting for someone. Let's listen in, shall we?

SONG #4: ANOTHER NIGHT AT THE PALACE.

ALL: **IT'S ANOTHER NIGHT AT THE PALACE
FOR THE ROYAL FAMILY.
ANOTHER NIGHT AT THE PALACE
AND WE'RE DRIPPING WITH NOBILITY.**

QUEEN: **THE JEWELS ARE IN THE CROWN.**

KING: **UNEMPLOYMENT RATE IS DOWN..**

PRINCESS: **I CAN'T STAND THIS GOWN!**

ALL: **IT'S ANOTHER NIGHT AT THE PALACE
FOR THE ROYAL FAMILY.
ANOTHER NIGHT AT THE PALACE**

	AND WE'RE DRIPPING WITH NOBILITY.
KING:	ANOTHER NIGHT AT THE PALACE AND ALL IS WELL WITH THE LAND THE DRAGON'S IN THE DUNGEON AND THE KNIGHTS ARE AT THEIR STANDS.
QUEEN:	ANOTHER NIGHT AT THE PALACE, SUCH CHARM, HOW QUAINT. ALTHOUGH IT SEEMS THE WALLS COULD USE A COAT OF PAINT!
PRINCESS:	IT'S ANOTHER NIGHT AT THE PALACE! I HATE THIS DRAFTY OLD PLACE. THE MOST EXCITING THING TO DO IS SIT AND FIX MY FACE!
ALL:	IT'S ANOTHER NIGHT, (ETC.) CODA: AND WE'RE DRIPPING, DRIPPING WITH NOBILITY!
PRINCESS:	(Sigh) Well, I guess I've kept them waiting long enough. I'll go down to dinner now. After all, Daddy did finally promise that I could go to Tahiti for school vacation.
AL:	(Appearing out of nowhere in the attire of the court) May I escort you, Princess?
PRINCESS:	What on…Who? What? Where did you come from?
AL:	I can answer ALL those questions. You see, I've just been appointed the new attaché to the King: your father, I believe. (To audience) I told you I had class.
PRINCESS:	Of all the….
AL:	Yes, isn't life strange? Shall we go?

THEY WALK ACROSS THE PROSCENIUM, PERHAPS INTO THE AUDIENCE AND ARRIVE AT THE DINING HALL

AL:	Your Highnesses, your daughter, the Princess. (the Princess just stands there. Al says sotto voce) I believe you're to curtsy, milady.
PRINCESS:	But I haven't curtsied to my parents in years!

AL: Have you forgotten how?

PRINCESS: Of course not!

AL: Then curtsy!

PRINCESS: Of all the!...HUMPF! (She curtsies.) There, how's that? (He/She pulls out her chair. She sits.)

AL: Perfectly lovely.

QUEEN: So, my dear, how was your day?

KING: Yes, dear, how was your day?

PRINCESS: The same as usual, Mother, Father. What's for dinner?

QUEEN: Let's see, the Chef has prepared the soup du jour, escargot, a salad…

PRINCESS: (Interrupting) Why can't we ever just have hamburgers and French Fries?

KING: That's a novel idea! Perhaps I should start a restaurant chain…I could call it…King's Burgers!!

PRINCESS: Oh, Father!

AL: (Entering) Excuse me, Your Excellencies.

KING: Yes, Aloysius/Alicia, what is it?

AL: Your dinner guest has arrived.

KING: Our dinner guest?

QUEEN: Oh no! Did you forget to tell me again?

KING: I'm not sure! Did you forget to tell me?

PRINCESS: (Popping up from the table.) Well, you NEVER tell me! You're both always springing these absurd little Prince characters on me. I don't know who did it this time, but I am NOT amused. I do NOT want to see another Prince!

AL:	Excuse me, Princess, but this guest says you invited him.
PRINCESS:	ME?? Why that's absurd! Why would I invite someone to dinner?
QUEEN:	Oh Princess, how exciting! Is he a Prince, or a Duke, or an Earl or a…
AL:	He's a frog.
QUEEN:	(Without missing a beat) or a FROG?!
PRINCESS:	Oh, NO!
KING:	Daughter, is there something we should know?
PRINCESS:	Oh, Daddy, it's nothing, really. Aloysius/Alicia, tell him to go away!
AL:	As you wish, Milady.
QUEEN:	Now, just a minute, I want to hear why there is a frog at our door saying he's been invited to dinner by our daughter. It sounds like a really good story!
KING:	Well, Princess, we are waiting.
PRINCESS:	(As fast as she can speak) Well, I was in my garden today playing with my gold ball and there was an ugly old frog there and he said my hair was mussed and I didn't have a mirror so I went over to the well to look at my reflection in the water and the ball fell in the stupid well, so the silly frog went down in the well to get my beautiful ball, but he wouldn't go in unless I promised him he could come to dinner and then sleep on a stupid silk pillow and so mmmmmmsssfapapdid.
KING & QUEEN:	(After a take to each other) And so WHAT?
PRINCESS:	And so mmmmmmmsssfapapdid.
KING:	Once more, please, slowly this time.
PRINCESS:	(Drawing a deep breath.) And so I did.
QUEEN:	And so you did what?
PRINCESS:	(Very reluctantly) I told him he could come to dinner…and that…

QUEEN: Yes?

PRINCESS: And that he could sleep on a stupid silk pillow. Now can we please tell him to go away?!

KING: Why ever would we do that?

PRINCESS: Because I don't want to have dinner with a frog!

KING: But you made a promise!

QUEEN: You know, dear, in my career I've had to have dinner with quite a few people whose company I really didn't enjoy, but nonetheless…

PRINCESS: But, Mother, he's not a person; he's a FROG!

QUEEN: But nonetheless, your father is right. A promise is a promise.

PRINCESS: But I'm a PRINCESS! I shouldn't have to keep promises.

KING: As you wish, daughter. You are a princess, and no one can force you to keep your word.

PRINCESS: That's right!

KING: Oh, by the way, I've changed my mind. You'll not be going to Tahiti for vacation this year.

PRINCESS: What?! How can you say that? You PROMISED!

QUEEN: But he's the King…

KING: That's right…I'm the King.

PRINCESS: The King, huh? Well, if you can't trust "The King" to keep his promise than (her voice trailing off) who can you trust?

THEY ALL DO A SERIES OF "TAKES" WITH ONE ANOTHER.

(Suddenly to Aloysius/Alicia) All right! Tell our "guest" to come in!!!

AL: Yes, Milady. (He/She leaves and reenters immediately with the

Frog Prince.) Your Highnesses, I present your guest, and my friend, Mr. Frog.

#5 *ROYAL FANFARE*

FP:	(Bowing low to the family) I can't tell you how honored I am to be here.
PRINCESS:	(Nastily) You should be!
KING:	So, Mr. Frog, tell me about yourself. You must have had some interesting experiences!
FP:	Well, sir, as a matter of fact I have. Why, I remember the time…(their voices fade)
QUEEN:	(Whispering to Princess.) You might as well try to be charming, dear. It won't serve any purpose to make everyone else miserable.
PRINCESS:	Charming?
QUEEN:	Isn't that right, Aloysius/Alicia?
AL:	Why yes, Milady. Have you forgotten how to be charming, Princess?
PRINCESS:	(Mimicking) Have I forgotten how to be charming? Of course not, you…
AL:	Then why don't you try it?
KING:	What a wonderful story, Mr. Frog. Oh Queen, Queen, Mr. Frog was just telling me about the time he…(His voice trails off.)
AL:	(Stepping out of the scene) And so the family had a rather enjoyable evening with a delightful dinner guest for a change. And the Princess tried her hardest to be charming.)
PRINCESS:	(In a very stilted voice.) Ha, ha. Oh. What "A" lovely story.
QUEEN:	(To Princess) Not bad, dear. Keep practicing.
AL:	There were only a few uncomfortable moments.
QUEEN:	Aloysius/Alicia! There's a fly in my soup!

FP:	Oh, Your Highness, you must have gotten MY bowl.
AL:	The other uncomfortable moment occurred when the evening was drawing to a close.
PRINCESS:	Well, I'm really tired now…so if you'll all excuse me…
FP:	Yes! Finally. Silk pillows!
PRINCESS:	Excuse me?
FP:	Silk pillows!
KING:	That's right. The other part of the promise.
PRINCESS:	Oh, come on now! You're not really going to HOLD me to that! Of all the…
KING:	I'm not really going to anything!
PRINCESS:	But Papa!
KING:	Just remember what I told you about promises. It's called the promise chain. I'm at the top of it, along with the Queen. You're next, and on and on. If one link in the promise chain is broken, the whole thing falls apart.
PRINCESS: QUEE QUEEN:	You make it sound so, so… Simple?
PRINCESS:	Yes, simple and, and
AL:	Important?
PRINCESS:	Yes, that too.
KING:	It is. Very important.
PRINCESS:	Could I just have a minute to think about all this?
KING:	Certainly, but just a minute. It's not polite to keep someone waiting.
PRINCESS:	Papa, he's a FROG!

KING: I'm well aware of what he is. Go on now.

LIGHTS FADE MUSIC STARTS.

PRINCESS: Let's see, "A" I should let him sleep on the pillow. Or "B" I should send him packing. Whoa, this is tough!

SONG #6: EENY MEENY

I MUST MAKE A DECISION BETWEEN "A" AND "B"
THIS ISN'T SOMETHING THAT COMES TO ME NATURALLY.
I SHOULD USE MORE PRECISION
IN MATTERS SUCH AS THESE.
BUT EENY MEENY MINEY MOH
HAS ALWAYS WORKED FOR ME.

EENY MEENY MINEY MOH,
THERE'S THIS FROG AND I DON'T KNOW
IF I OUGHT TO MAKE HIM GO,
EENY MEENY MINEY MOH.

(REPEAT)

I PR0MISED I WOULD LET HIM STAY.
BUT I DON'T WANT TO.
IT'S THE RIGHT THING TO DO.
BUT I DON'T WANT TO.
I DON'T KNOW IF I OUGHT TO MAKE HIM GO.
EENY MEENY MINEY MOH.

EVERYONE WILL BE UPSET IF I DON'T.
BUT I DON'T WANT TO.
HE'S NOT SO BAD.
BUT I DON'T WANT TO.

EENY MEENY MINEY MOH,
THERE'S THIS FROG AND I DON'T KNOW
IF I OUGHT TO MAKE HIM GO.
EENY MEENY MINEY MOH.
EENY MEENY MINEY MOH.
EENY MEENY MINEY MOH.

(SPOKEN) HE STAYS.

SCENE CHANGE DURING SONG. IN THE BACKGROUND THE FROG IS SEEN IN THE PRINCESS'S ROOM, PACING. HE FINALLY SITS ON THE PILLOW AT THE END OF THE SONG

SCENE 4 The Princess's bedroom

AL: So the Princess traveled the long dark hallways to her bedroom. When she opened the door to her chambers, the frog was already there, sitting comfortably on a large silk pillow.

PRINCESS: Well, Mr. Frog, (Sarcastically) I hope you're comfortable.

FP: Oh, I'm in heaven, thank you. Great room.

PRINCESS: Now go to sleep.

FP: Thank you, I will. Aren't you going to sleep?

PRINCESS: No.

FP: Why not?

PRINCESS: That's really none of your business!

FP: I guess it's not.

PRINCESS: (Really wanting to tell him.) I mean, why should I tell YOU?

FP: It couldn't hurt!

PRINCESS: Oh, all right, if you insist. The fact is; I don't sleep well at night.

FP: Really?

PRINCESS: Really. I've never told anyone this before, and I really don't know why I'm telling you…but (stage whispering) I'm afraid of the dark.

FP: Hmmmmm.

PRINCESS: Well, aren't you going to laugh?

FP: Why would I do that? That wouldn't be very nice.

PRINCESS: Because it's absurd! A PRINCESS afraid of the dark! How ridiculous!

FP:	You know, it's nothing to be ashamed of. A lot of people are afraid of the dark. A lot of frogs are too!
PRINCESS:	Is that so?
FP:	Why yes! Say, would it help if I told you a story? I'm very good at it, you know.
PRINCESS:	I'm sure you are. All right, if you insist. Go ahead. Tell me a story.
FP:	Well, once upon a time…
AL:	(From the side) And so the frog told the Princess a beautiful story and by the time he said "The End," she was sound asleep.
FP:	"The End." (Yawning) Good night Princess.
AL:	Good night Princess. Goodnight my friend.

BLACKOUT, THEN LIGHTS UP HALF

AL:	And so they slept. (SFX snore sounds) Each with their own dreams, each touched by faint memories of childhood. And into these memories crept the strange image of a woman long ago. (Sounds of FGM stumbling into the room)
FGM:	Oo, ow, ooch, owch. Mercy! Doesn't anyone use nightlights anymore? Hey kids, remember me? That's right, the Fairy Godmother! I'll be you've been wondering where I've been. Well, haven't you? Oh, all right, so you forgot all about me. Well, I'll tell you what I've been doing anyway. I've been keeping my eye on things, that's what. After all, one of these "characters" is still my godchild. Even is he IS a frog! Isn't it interesting what a nice "person" my frog turned out to be, and what a spoiled brat the human princess became! Go figure!
	And just so you know, I'm not MAD anymore. So I didn't get invited to a party! Big deal! Took a few years and some intense therapy, but I think I'm over it now!
	Well, I know you can't wait to get back to the story. But let's see if maybe I can complicate things a bit. I'll just take my little Frog Prince with me! And what should I do with him? Change him back into a human? That would be interesting, wouldn't it? Let's see, Flibbity gibbitt, gibbitty doo, have I ever got plans for you!

Arise from your pillow and walk in your sleep. We have places to go and promises to keep. (The Prince gets up and follows her.)

PRINCE: (As he rises) Places to go and promises to keep…Places to go and promises to keep…Robert Frost?

FGM: That's "miles to go before I sleep," dear. Watch your step. It's dark in here.

PRINCE: Carl Sandburg??? Places to go, promises to keep. Places (trailing off)

PRINCESS: (Waking up, yawning, stretching.) Oh my! I haven't slept that well in…As a matter of fact, I've never slept that well!!! I feel wonderful!

KING: (Entering nervously.) Good morning dear, how are we this…

PRINCESS: Oh, Father, I'm great this morning! I feel like a new person!

KING: Oh my, Are you sick? Let me feel your forehead.

PRINCESS: (Laughing) Papa, I'm fine, really. Couldn't be better!

KING: And you're in such a good mood!

PRINCESS: Yes! I told you, I feel great! And for that I can thank the creature who slept on my silk pillow! He told me a wonderful bedtime story, and he was so kind to me, I forgot to be afraid. My friend Mr. (She looks around and sees that he is gone.) Oh, no! Mr. Frog! Where is he? Where did he go? Papa help me!

(They both frantically search for the frog. Ad libs)

QUEEN: (Entering) What's going on?

PRINCESS: Oh, Mama, he's gone!

QUEEN: Who's gone?

PRINCESS: Why, the frog, of course!

QUEEN: Of course, of course. Well, aren't you glad?

PRINCESS: No, Mama! I've got to find him! (She runs out.)

QUEEN: Now she likes the frog? Am I missing something here?

KING: Yes. A lot. Come on, I'll fill you in.

SCENE 5: THE GARDEN

AL: And so I, Aloysius/Alicia T. Frog waited in the garden. It only made sense that the Princess would come to the place where she had first met this peculiar creature.

PRINCESS: Please be here, Froggie, please, please. (She stops and looks quietly around.) Look, I have my gold ball. We can play catch!

AL: Hello Milady.

PRINCESS: Oh, Mr. Frog, I knew I'd find…Oh, it's only you.

AL: Yes, it is only I. Whom were you expecting?

PRINCESS: No one. No one in particular.

AL: Well, then, I just came to tell you that your parents are worried about you.

PRINCESS: You can tell them not to worry. I'm fine.

AL: All right. I'll tell them that.

PRINCESS: Wait a minute.

AL: Yes?

PRINCESS: Would you like to play catch?

AL: With a frog?

PRINCESS: No, with a ball, silly.

AL: I'd love to.

SONG #7: A GOLDEN BALL

PRINCESS: **SAILING LIKE THE MOON
FLOATING IN THE AIR**

AL; **LIKE A FERRIS WHEEL
AT A COUNTY FAIR.**

PRINCESS: **IT'S NOTHING LIKE A DIAMOND
MORE LIKE A PEARL**

BOTH: **ROUND AND SHINY,
SOMETHING LIKE THE WORLD.**

AL: **WHAT IF TWO GIANTS ARE PLAY8NG AFTER WORK,
TOSSING THEIR BALL,
BUT THEIR BALL IS WHAT WE CALL EARH?**

PRINCESS: **DO YOU THINK THEY'D NOTICE US?
I WONDER IF THEY'D CARE,**

BOTH: **THAT WE'RE THE LITTLE PEOPLE THEY'RE TOSSING
THROUGH THE AIR!**

**LIKE "HORTON HEARS A WHO!", IS IT POSSIBLE THAT YOU
AND I ARE BEING CARRIED BY SOME KINDLY CREATURE
FROM ANOTHER WORLD?**

SAILING LIKE THE MOON,

AL: **FLOATING IN THE AIR.**

PRINCESS: **LIKE A FERRIS WHEEL**

AL: **AT A COUNTY FAIR.**

PRINCESS: **IT'S NOTHING LIKE A DIAMOND,**

AL: **MORE LIKE A PEARL.**

BOTH: **ROUND AND SHINY,**

SOMETHING LIKE THE WORLD.

AL: (Song ends) May I escort you home now?

PRINCESS: No. No thank you. I'll be staying here. Just in case he comes back.

AL: He?

PRINCESS: You know, your friend.

AL: Why are you waiting for him? I thought you'd be happy to see him go.

PRINCESS: So did I. But when I woke up this morning and he was gone, I had this really empty feeling inside.

AL: (Joking) Maybe you were hungry.

PRINCESS: Don't make fun. I'm serious. I'm going to stay here.

AL: I'm sorry for making fun, but it's getting dark. And you'll be cold.

PRINCESS: I'll be all right, don't worry.

AL: I'll bring you a blanket.

PRINCESS: Thank you. You are too kind.

AL: You're thanking me?

PRINCESS: Why yes, I guess I am.

AL: You know, Princess, you've changed.

PRINCESS: I have, haven't I? Isn't life strange?

AL: Yes, isn't it?

AL: (Covering her with a blanket.) And so the Princess slept in her little garden hoping her Frog would appear. He didn't. The next morning her mother and father came to try to persuade her to come back to the castle.

KING: (Calling) Princess! Princess! Oh, look dear. Here she is. Princess! You must come back to the castle!

QUEEN:	You're going to catch pneumonia out here!
PRINCESS:	I'm fine, Mother. I'm fine, Father. Really, don't worry about me!
KING:	But we DO worry about you! It's our job to worry about you!
QUEEN:	For instance, I worry about you sleeping on this bench!
PRINCESS:	I slept very well on this bench.
KING:	And I worry about the night air.
PRINCESS:	The night air was beautiful!
QUEEN:	I worry that you'll be (whispering) frightened in the dark!
PRINCESS:	But I wasn't frightened, Mother. Not at all.
KING:	Well, I worry about…what else can we worry about, Queen?
QUEEN:	I can't think of anything right now, but I'll keep trying.
PRINCESS:	There, now both of you, stop worrying. If he doesn't come back in two days, I'll come back to the castle!
KING:	Two days?! That's a long time.
PRINCESS:	Not so very long, Father. But I'll come back sooner if he appears.
KING:	Is that a promise?
PRINCESS:	A promise? Yes, that's a promise.
QUEEN:	(Getting teary) All right, dear. We'll see you in a day or two. Come on King. There's nothing more we can do here. We'll return to the palace.
KING:	(As he and Queen exit.) Yes, Queen. Oh, our little Princess is growing up.
	(Princess starts to play with her ball, humming to herself. A young man enters. It is the Prince.)
PRINCE:	Hello.
PRINCESS:	Oh! You startled me!

PRINCE: I'm sorry.

PRINCESS: Who are you anyway?

PRINCE: Well, (rather unsure of himself) I'm told I'm a Prince.

PRINCESS: A Prince, huh? Well, that's nice.

PRINCE: I suppose. Is this your garden?

PRINCESS: Yes, it is.

PRINCE: Sorry, I must have wandered from the main road. I can leave.

PRINCESS: You don't have to. I'm just waiting.

PRINCE: Waiting? For someone?

PRINCESS: Um, kind of. For a frog.

PRINCE: Oh, you have a pet frog?

PRINCESS: No, no, no. more like a (trying the word out)…friend.

PRINCE: Oh, you're waiting for a friend. That's nice.

PRINCESS: Actually, oh, never mind. Say, what kind of Prince are you anyway? I've never seen you before.

FP: I was afraid you'd ask that. I'm not quite sure. You see I don't remember much. As a matter of fact, I don't remember anything.

PRINCESS: You're weird.

FP: Am I? Is that bad?

PRINCESS: I'm sorry. I shouldn't have called you weird.

FP: That's all right. (To audience) I guess it was bad.

PRINCESS: Say, do you want to play catch?

FP: With a Prince?

PRINCESS: No, with a ball, of course.

FP:	I've never played catch before. I'm not sure I know how!
PRINCESS:	I'll teach you.
FP:	Okay.

SONG #8: FRIENDS

PRINCE:	**I'VE SO MUCH TO LEARN THIS IS ALL SO NEW. TOSSING A BALL WITH SOMEONE LIKE YOU.**
PRINCESS:	**WE COULD BE FRIENDS. I'VE NEVER HAD A FRIEND BEFORE. I WONDER WHAT IT'S LIKE.**
PRINCE:	**WE COULD BE FRIENDS!**
BOTH:	**I THINK IT WOULD BE NICE!**
PRINCE:	**LIKE THE JACK WHO FOUND HIS JILL, IS IT POSSIBLE THAT WE'LL BE FRIENDS BEFORE THE ENDING OF A PERFECT GAME WITH THIS GOLDEN BALL?**
BOTH:	**SAILING LIKE THE MOON,**
PRINCE:	**FLOATING IN THE AIR**
PRINCESS:	**LIKE THE FERRIS WHEEL**
PRINCE:	**AT THE COUNTY FAIR.**
PRINCESS:	**IT'S NOTHING LIKE A DIAMOND,**
PRINCE:	**MORE LIKE A PEARL.**
BOTH:	**ROUND AND SHINY. SOMETHING LIKE THE WORLD.**
	AT THE END OF THE SONG THE BALL FALLS IN THE WELL.
PRINCESS:	Oh no! Not again! My beautiful ball!
PRINCE:	I'm so sorry. I'll get it for you.

PRINCESS:	How are you going to do that? You're not a …frog!
PRINCE:	No, I'm not. At least I don't think I am. And I think I'm having déjà vu, but nevertheless, I can get if for you.
PRINCESS:	I can't let you do that..
PRINCE:	Why not?
PRINCESS:	(Melodramatically) A gold ball is not worth any danger that might befall you!
PRINCE:	Wow. That's intense.
PRINCESS:	I'm serious. It's just a ball. I don't need it.

A RUMBLING IS HEARD AND THEN A PUFF OF SMOKE. THE FAIRY GODMOTHER APPEARS. SHE IS CARRYING THE GOLD BALL.

FGM:	POOF! Yoohoo! Is this the ball you're talking about?
PRINCESS:	Who are you? How did you…?
PRINCE:	Not YOU again!
PRINCESS:	You know her?
PRINCE:	All I know is, every time I see her my whole life gets turned upside down!
FGM:	I promise I won't do any more turning upside-down stuff.
PRINCE:	You promise?
FGM:	I said I promise.
PRINCESS:	And a promise is a promise. Now who are you and what is going on?
FGM:	Well, in a nutshell, I'm HIS fairy godmother, I got mad when he was a baby, turned him into a frog and the spell could only be broken if he convinced a princess to let him share her dinner with him and allow him to sleep on a silk pillow.

PRINCESS: (To Prince) YOU??!!

PRINCE: It's beginning to come back to me!

PRINCESS: YOU??!!

PRINCE: The golden ball, the well…

PRINCESS: YOU??!!

FGM: Can't you say anything else besides YOU??!! Listen, Prince, I hope I've cleared things up for you.

PRINCE: Well, I'm not sure yet. But you won't forget your promise, will you?

FGM: I won't forget! I promise! I promise! Oh, Princess, here's your ball.

PRINCESS: YOU??!! Oh, sorry, sorry. I won't say that again. But I'm so confused!

PRINCE: YOU'RE confused! You haven't been a frog your whole life!

PRINCESS: Well, that's true. Oh, look who's here. (Aloysius/Alicia enters humming "Lily Pad Heaven.") Aloysius/Alicia, you'll never believe…

PRINCE: (To Al) Wait a minute. I think I know you!

AL: (Walks around Prince checking him out.) So, it finally happened, eh?

PRINCE: I do know you! You're my friend! My friend, Al.

PRINCESS: You mean you knew about this?

AL: I was there. You were both babies!

PRINCE: We knew each other when we were babies?

AL: Not only that! You knew each other when you were a frog!

PRINCESS: Not only that. We knew each other when I was a…well, when I was not a very nice person.

AL: But that's all changed now, isn't it?

PRINCESS: Yes, yes it is…all changed.

SCENE 6

KING AND QUEEN ENTER.

KING & QUEEN: Princess…Oh, Princess! We just couldn't stay away.

PRINCESS: Mother, Father, I'd like you to meet a friend of mine.

QUEEN: (Gushing) Oh, our little Princess is really growing up! And this uh…lovely lady…why you must be this young man's mother!

FGM: Well, uh, actually, well, uh, sort of…yes! A mother of sorts. Nice to meet you.

PRINCESS: And would it be all right, Father and Mother, if I invited him, uh, them to dinner?

KING: Of course, dear. It would be a pleasure. But what about the friend you were waiting for?

PRINCESS: Mr. Frog? Hmmm. I think I found him.

KING: You have eh? Well, all right, if you say so. Anyway, it's a pleasure to meet you ma'am. And you, young man.

PRINCE: (Bowing graciously) The pleasure is all mine, Your Highnesses.

QUEEN: (Still gushing. To Princess.) Oooo. He's nice dear, very nice.

AL: Two nice young people! (Music starts)

KING: Our daughter—Nice? Well, yes, I guess she is, now isn't she?

PRINCESS: And I tell you what.

AL: (Sings) **SOMETIMES A PROMISE…**

PRINCESS: (continuing) I promise…always to try to be nice, and not selfish and nasty like I used to be.

QUEEN: Oh, that's good daughter, so good.

QUEEN & AL:	(Sing) **SOMETIMES A PROMISE…**
PRINCESS:	And one more thing.
KING:	What's that?
PRINCESS:	I, Princess, promise never to break a promise!
KING, QUEEN & AL:	**SOMETIMES A PROMISE…**
PRINCE:	Isn't life strange, Aloysius?
AL:	Yes. Isn't it?

SONG #9: SOMETIMES A PROMISE

AL:	**SOMETIMES A PROMISE CAN MAKE THE WORLD A BETTER PLACE.**
PRINCE:	**SOMETIMES A PROMISE BRINGS A SMILE TO SOMEONE'S FACE.**
PRINCESS:	**SOMETIMES A PROMISE MEANS MORE THAN YOU THOUGHT IT WOULD.**
ALL:	**BUT ALWAYS A PROMISE "KEPT" IS SOMETHING GOOD.**
	PROMISES MEAN EVERYTHING TO SOMEONE WHO'S COUNTING ON THEM.
	KEEPING A PROMISE MEANS YOU CAN COUNT ON THEM TOO!
	SOMETIMES A PROMISE.
	SOMETIMES A PROMISE.
	SOMETIMES A PROMISE MEANS MORE THAN YOU THOUGHT IT WOULD.
	BUT ALWAYS A PROMISE "KEPT" IS SOMETHING GOOD!
	(REPEAT.)

THE END

MUSIC FROM
THE FROG PRINCE
BY
JAN CALLNER

Cover Art by Christine Boyka Kluge

Copyright 1995, 2022, 2025

Jan Callner

Mike and Me Productions

MUSIC FROM THE FROG PRINCE BY JAN CALLNER

Song:

#1 Lily Pad Heaven Prelude

#2 The Mad Song

#3 Lily Pad Heaven

#4 Another Night at the Palace

#5 Royal Fanfare

#6 Eeny Meeny

#7 The Golden Ball

#8 Friends

#9 Sometimes a Promise

Lily Pad Heaven

#1

Our narrator, Aloysius T. Frog, sings his theme song.

Words and Music
by Jan Callner

copyright 1995

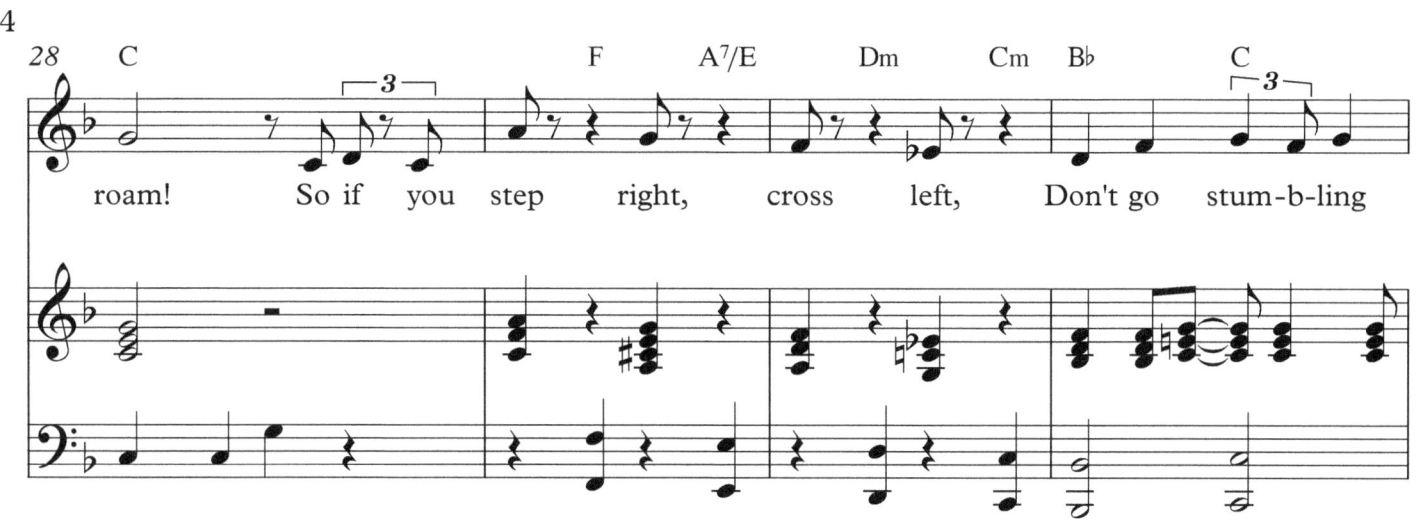
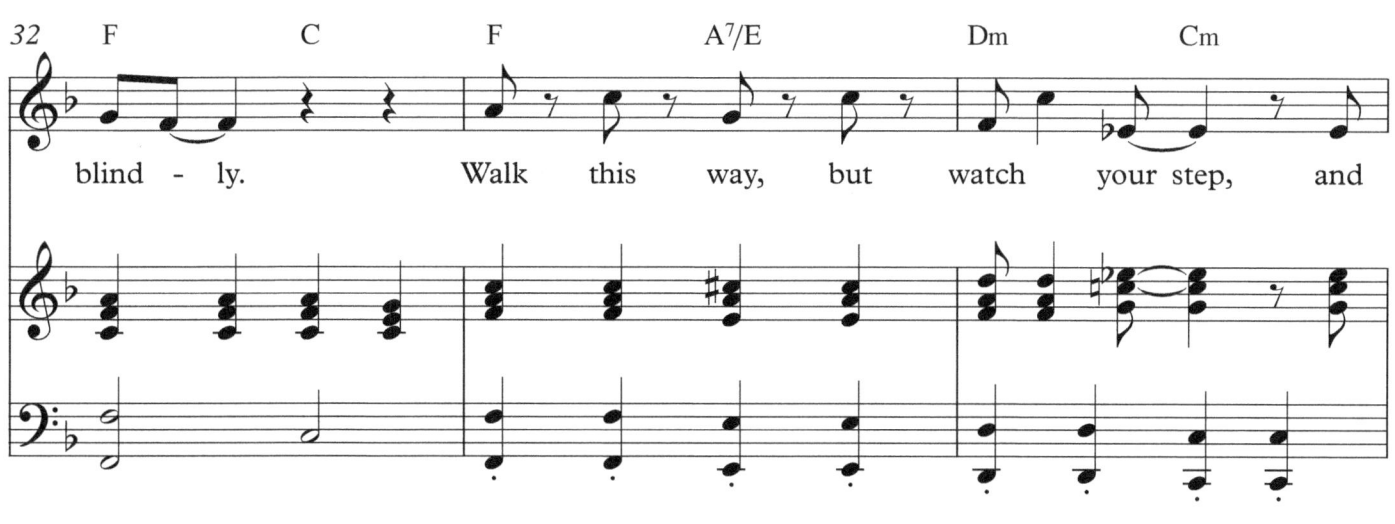
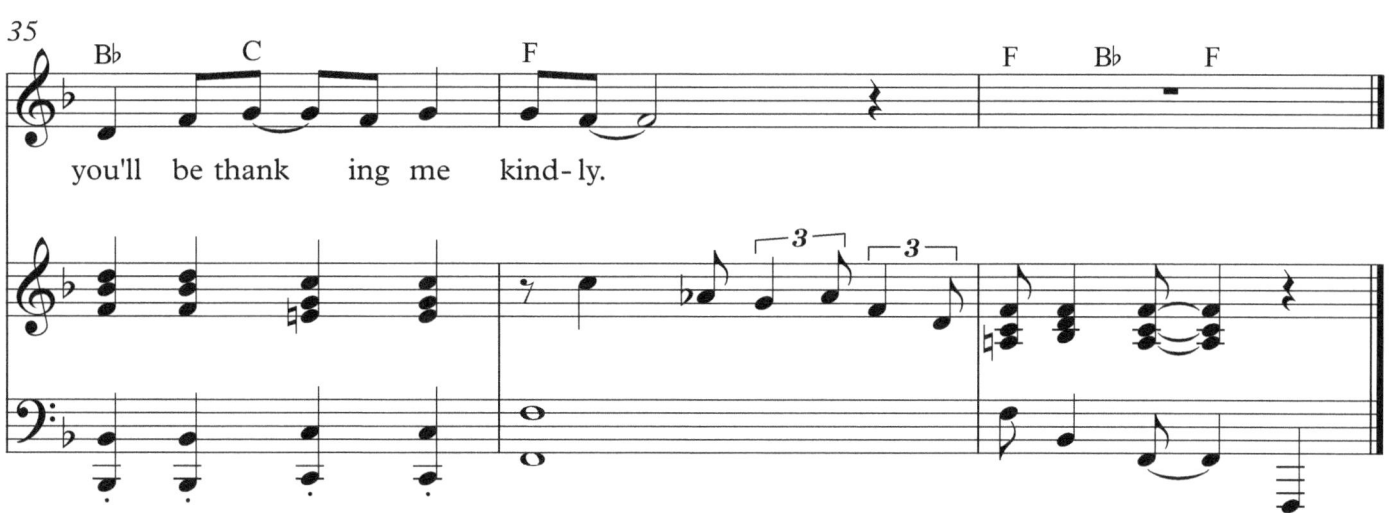

The Mad Song

The King and Queen have forgotten to invite the Prince's Fairygodmother to his first birthday party. She is not happy to have been left out.

Words and Music by Jan Callner

copyright 1995

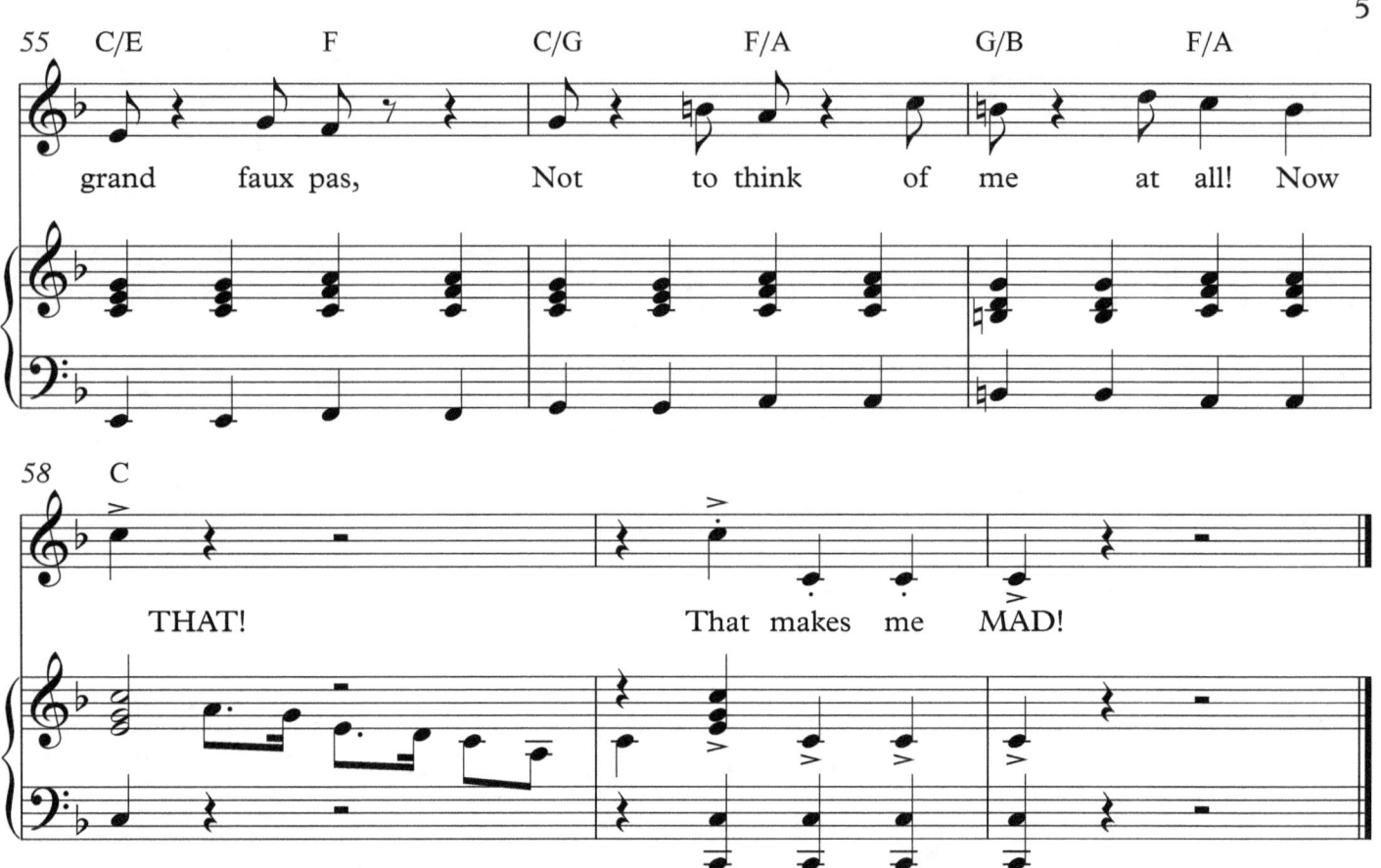

While the baby Prince and Princess are playing, the Fairygodmother joins them in the garden. The Princess runs to hide before the Fairygodmother casts a spell over the Prince--which she does--and she turns him into a frog!

The Princess comes out from hiding just as her father, the King, enters.
He consoles his daughter who is surprised to see a frog instead of a baby Prince. The King tells her a frog is nothing to be afraid of and they leave.

Aloysius T. Frog appears and takes the younger frog under his care to teach him the ways of his "kind."

Lily Pad Heaven

#3

Aloysius T. Frog must teach his new friend the ways of a frog. Like where the juciest flies are and how to find the best lily pads.

Words and Music by Jan Callner

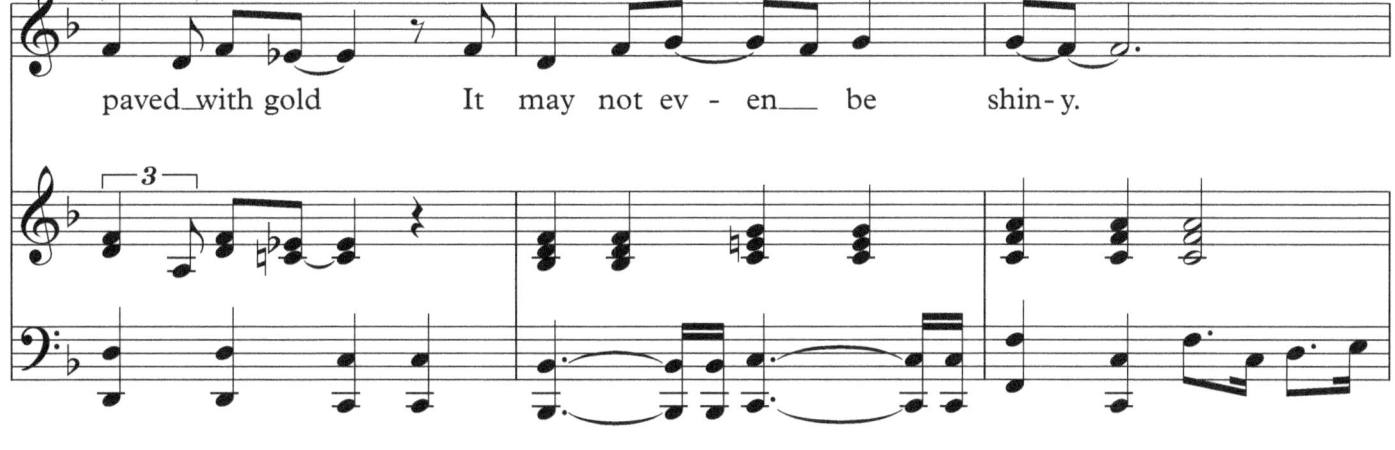
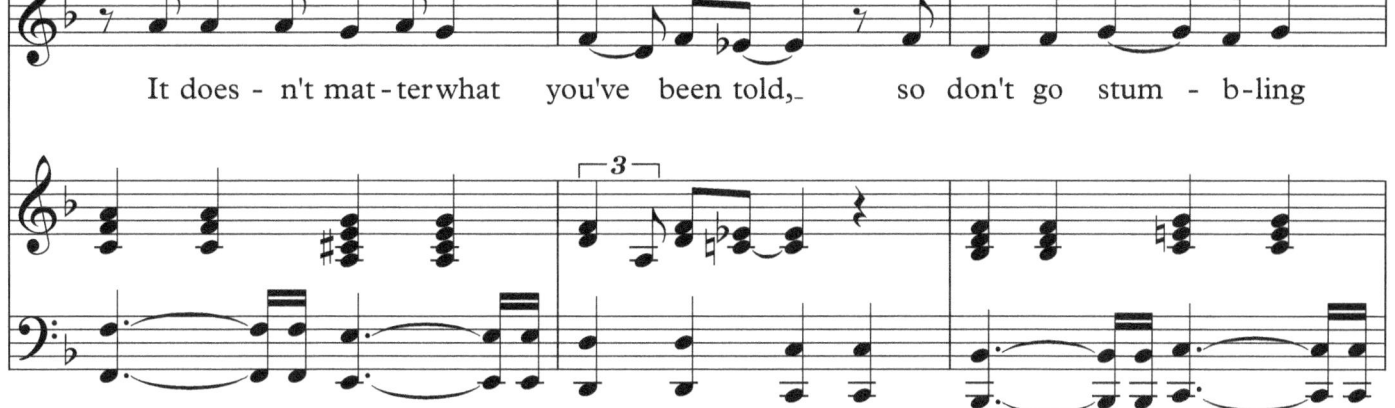

copyright 1995

Another Night At the Palace

#4

It is eighteen years later.
The King and Queen are waiting at the dinner table for their unpleasant daughter, the
Princess. The couple seem happy with their lives, the Princess not so much.

Words and Music
by Jan Callner

ALL: It's an-oth-er night at the pal-ace

for the roy-al fam-i-ly. An-oth-er night at the pal-ace and we're drip-ping with no

bil-i-ty. QUEEN: The jewels are in the crown! KING: Un-em-ploy-ment rate is

Copyright © 1995

The Princess thought she'd had a hard day. In the afternoon she had been playing in her garden with her beautiful golden ball while also admiring her own beauty, when she spotted a large frog eating lunch. He told her her hair looked a little mussed.

She ran to the well so she could see her reflection in the water, and the ball fell in!

She convinced the frog to retrieve it for her by promising he could dine at the palace and sleep on silk pillows.

The frog shows up and shares a lovely dinner with the King and Queen.

The Princess is not happy, and she has no intention of letting the frog sleep on her silk pillows.
Her parents remind her of how important it is to keep promises.

Royal Fanfare

#5

Music
Jan Callner

Eeny Meeny

The Princess leaves the dinner table and walks slowly to her room. She struggles to make a decision about the kindly frog who had helped her.

Words and Music
by Jan Callner

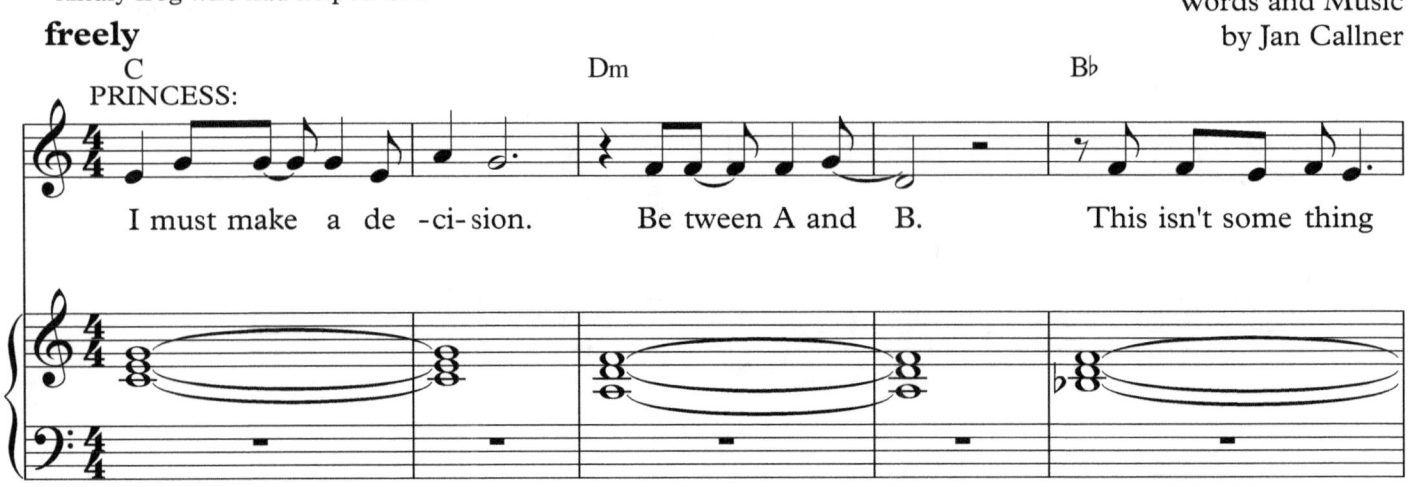

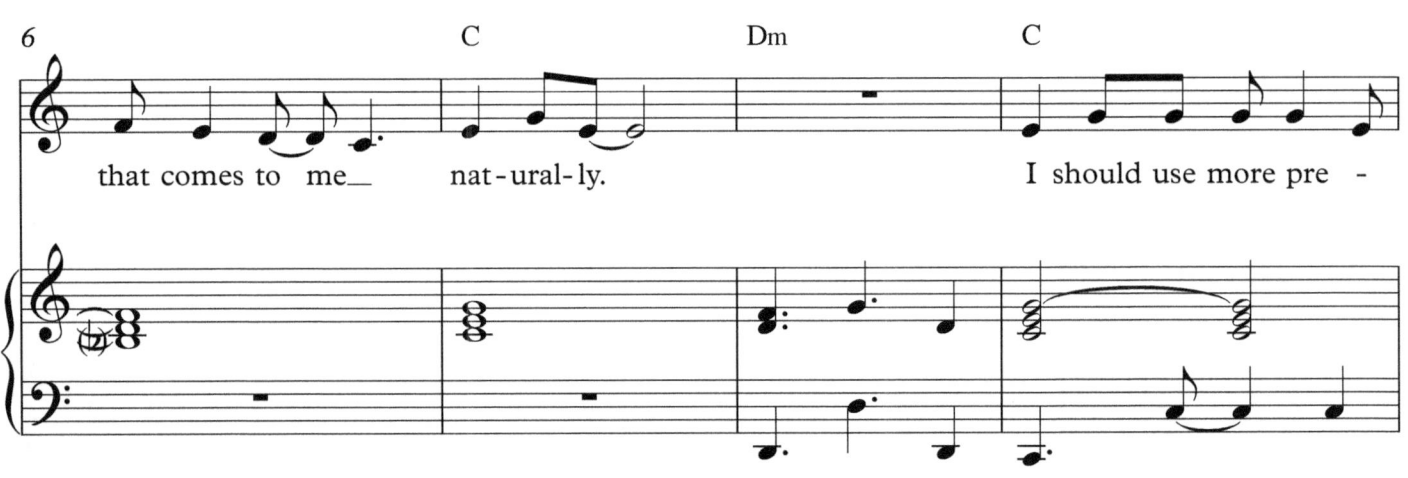

copyright 1995

At the end of the song, the Princess tells Aloysius she's going to continue to wait for her friend. Al offers to bring her a blanket. She says, "No, I'll be fine, but thank you." The Princess had never thanked anyone before. Aloysius tells her she's changed. She realizes he's right.

Friends

#8

The Princess is waiting for her friend when a young man appears, startling her. She asks him to play catch with her Golden Ball. He says he doesn't know how.
"I'll teach you!" she says.

Words and Music by Jan Callner

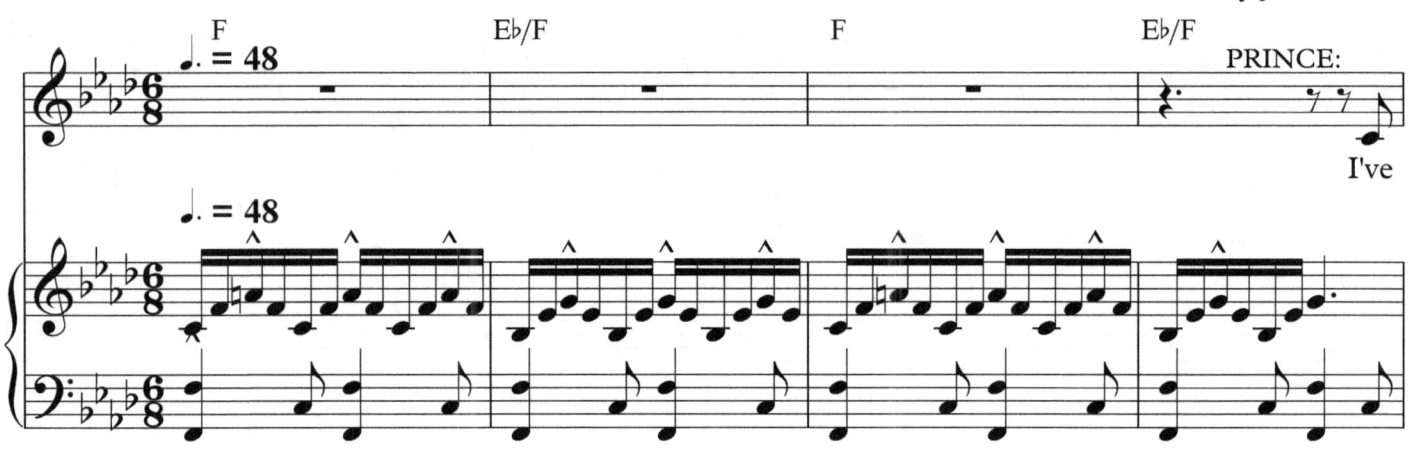

copyright 1995

At the end of the song, the ball falls into the well...AGAIN. The Prince offers to retrieve it.
Out of nowhere the Fairygodmother appears with the Golden Ball. They figure out it was she who cast a spell. The two young people had really known each other since they were babies!

Sometimes A Promise

#9

So the Prince discovers he used to be a frog, and the Princess realizes he is the friend she's been looking for. They have found each other again!

The Princess promises not to be selfish anymore and to always keep a promise! Everyone sings the final song.

Words and Music by Jan Callner

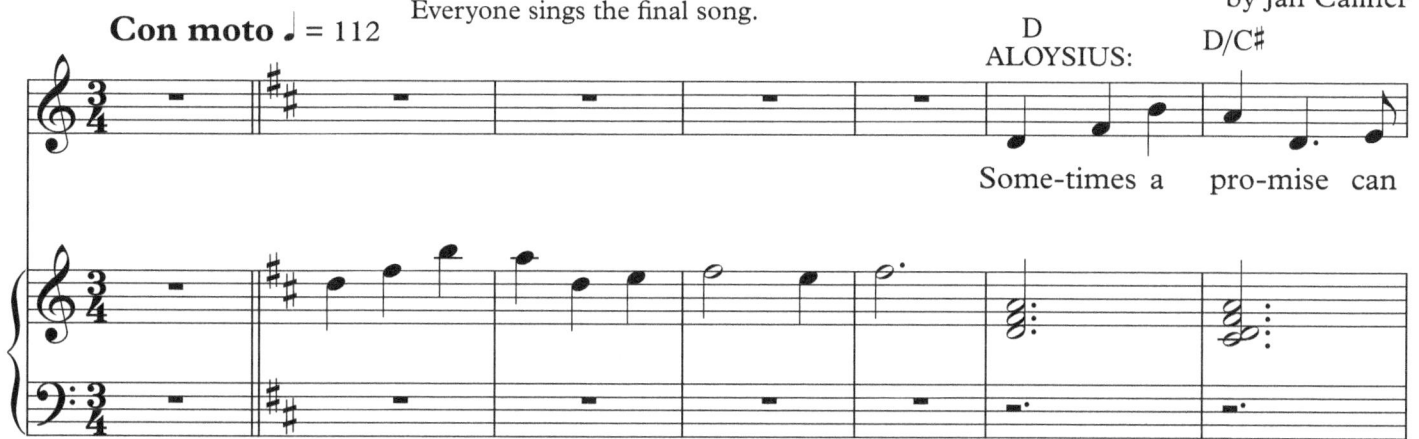

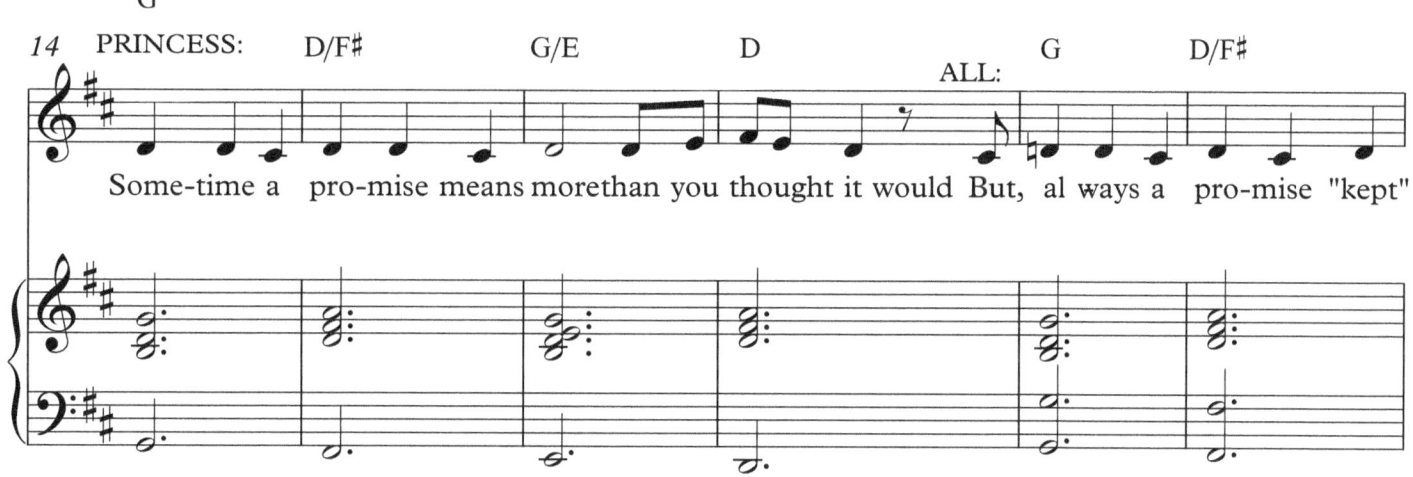

Copyright © 1995

NOW SHE *LIKES* THE FROG?

Thank you for letting us come to the show. This is when the princess drop the gold ball in the well. "Oh Froggy, maybe you can get it." Mia Kara

Thank you for coming to our school and performing "The Frog Prince". My favorite part was when something fell into the well and they made noise like Look, Look I am Swiming

from,
Anthony E.

Chosen as a winner of the
Early Childhood News
2000 Directors' Choice Awards

The Frog Prince
Mike and Me Productions/Callner Kids

THE MAGIC FISH

A One-Act

Musical for Children

Cover Art by Christine Boyke Kluge

Script by Jan Callner & Bill Wheeler

Music & Lyrics by Jan Callner

Copyright 1998, 2014, 2025

Jan Callner

Mike and Me Productions

Characters

Bert/Bertie	A Pelican: Companion to the Fisherman
The Fisherman	Congenial man susceptible to influence
The Wife	Pie maven, wishful thinker
The Fish	Talented sea creature with powers

Scenes

Scene 1	Oceanside. Fishnet, piling, etc. A seaside hut
Scene 2	Oceanside with large wave
Scene 3	Seaside hut
Scene 4	Oceanside with wave
Scene 5	Little cottage
Scene 6	Stormy ocean
Scene 7	A Mansion
Scene 8	Ocean
Scene 9	A Castle
Scene 10	Raging Ocean
Scene 11	Little hut

Set

S.R. Pilings and fish nets, S.L. Ocean Wave, Center Stage a large set cube that can be turned on wheels. First side is a little hut, Second side is a cottage, Third side is a mansion, Fourth side is a castle

Songs

1. I Am A Pel-I-Can — Bert/Bertie
2. Little Hut by the Sea — Fisherman/Wife
3. I Couldn't Be an Octopus — The Fish
4. Just One Wish — The Wife
5. Good Husband — The Fisherman
6. Minor Masterpiece — Instrumental
7. Royal Music — Instrumental
8. What Do You Do?   (In two keys) — Bert/Bertie
9. The Sun and Moon Dance/Confusion — Instrumental
10. The Day Was Night — Fisherman/Wife/Fish
11. Dvorak's Largo — Instrumental
12. Little Hut Reprise — All
13. The Sea Can Be Magic — All

THE MAGIC FISH

Scene 1

LIGHTS UP ON A LITTLE SEASIDE HUT. THERE ARE SEVERAL PILINGS AROUND UPON WHICH A PELICAN MIGHT ROOST. MUSIC BEGINS. THERE IS A PELICAN ON STAGE.

SONG #1. I AM A PEL-I-CAN   (Pronounced Pel-EYE-Can)

WELCOME TO MY WORLD
HERE AT THE OCEAN.
I SWIM IN THE WATER,
I WALK ON THE SAND, FOR

I AM A PEL-I-CAN. I AM A PEL-I-CAN.
FOR I CAN SING, I CAN
AND I CAN TALK, I CAN,
AND I CAN SQUAWK, CAUSE
AFTER ALL, I AM A PEL-I-CAN!

A PELICAN IS A KIND OF BIRD,
OFTEN SEEN BUT SELDOM HEARD,
WITH A GIANT BEAK AND
TWO WEBBED FEET,
AND A HEART OF GOLD,
OR SO I'M TOLD.

I AM A PEL-I-CAN. I AM A PEL-I-CAN.
I CAN SING, AND
I CAN TALK, AND
I CAN SQUAWK, CAUSE
I'M A PELICAN!

(MUSICAL BREAK)

YES, I AM…A PEL-I CAN!

PELICAN: (Continues) Yessireee…A Pelican I am…and what this pelican needs now is breakfast! And my breakfast choice is…PIE! Yep, PIE. There's nothing I like better than fresh-baked…(Sniff) What's this? I think I'm on the right track! Could it be? Is today my lucky day! Do I spy a pie? Oooo, I rhymed! (Sniff) Yep, it's a pie all right! I think I'll just take me a nice big…

(Door slams, Wife enters)

Oh, oh, trouble.

WIFE: What do you think you're doing? Give me that pie. I said, "GIVE ME THAT…(they struggle SFX SQUISH) Ohhhh! Not like that…now look at me! These stains better come out or there will be one sorry pelican!

(The Fisherman enters whistling a happy tune.)

F.MAN: Oh wife…WOW. What happened to you?

WIFE: This pelican, and that pie, and my dress, and oh, never mind. I'm going to change my clothes. (She goes inside.)

F.MAN: Hi Bertie!

BERTIE: Hi Fisherman.

F.MAN: Sounds like you're in trouble.

BERTIE: I guess I am.

F.MAN: Don't worry, she'll get over it. Now would you give me a hand here?

BERTIE: What are you doing?

F.MAN: I'm trying to get my fishing lines untangled. They're a mess. Anything you'd like to tell me about that?

BERTIE: I guess I didn't do a very good job untangling.

F.MAN: No, but that's all right. I think I've got it now. Do you want to go with me?

BERTIE: I guess you're going fishing?

F.MAN: You guessed right. I've got to catch dinner. If I don't, there won't be anything but squished pie to eat.

BERTIE: Make me feel bad, why don't you?

F.MAN: Don't feel bad…I like squished pie. Especially apple cherry berry.

(Wife enters)

Here she is. There now, Wife, you look better.

WIFE: I should hope so. Now, dear husband, when you get back from fishing could you give the door on our hut a coat of paint? It really looks shabby.

F.MAN: It does, doesn't it?

WIFE: It's too bad you have to paint the house every year.

F.MAN: I know, but living on the ocean makes the paint peel. If only we had aluminum siding.

WIFE: Well, since we don't, a little paint will have to do.

F.MAN: Absolutely. I'd do anything for you, dear.

WIFE: Now don't go getting mushy on me.

F.MAN: I can't help it. This is the life!

SONG #2 LITTLE HUT BY THE SEA

F.MAN: **IN A HAPPY HUT BY THE SEA,**
WHERE WE LIVE, YOU AND ME.
IT ISN'T MUCH, BUT WE'RE HAPPY
HERE IN OUR LITTLE HUT BY THE SEA.
WE HAVE A ROOF TO KEEP US DRY
FOUR WALLS WHEN THE WIND GETS HIGH.
WE CAN SIT IN OUR LITTLE HUT BY THE SEA.
HAPPY HERE JUST YOU AND ME.

(He speaks) Come on now, sing with me before I go!

WIFE: If you insist.

WIFE: **IN OUR HAPPY HUT BY THE SEA**
F.MAN: **WHERE WE LIVE, YOU AND ME.**
WIFE: **IT ISN'T MUCH, BUT WE'RE HAPPY,**
BOTH: **HERE IN OUR LITTLE HUT BY THE SEA.**

WIFE: Off with you now, and catch a great fish, husband.

F.MAN: I'll do my best!

WIFE: And take that pelican with you!

F.MAN: We're going, we're going!

MUSICAL TAG, LIGHTS FADE, OCEAN SOUNDS, LIGHTS BACK UP

SCENE 2   THE OCEAN

BERTIE: SQUAWK! Beautiful day, eh?

F.MAN: Couldn't ask for better.

BERTIE: Blue sky, blue water, white sand! Yessiree, a fine day for fishing. Why I think it's one of the finest in a long time. I bet you're going to catch a lot of fish today, Fisherman. Why I would go so far as to say…

F.MAN: Why I think maybe you've said plenty already, my friend. You might scare the fish AWAY! And why is it you only speak to me and not to my good wife?

BERTIE: Well, to tell the truth, I don't think she would like to listen to me.

F.MAN: (Laughing) You may be right.

BERTIE: I thought you'd agree. So should we cast the lines out?

F.MAN: I'll cast the lines out. You always seem to get tangled up in something somehow.

BERTIE: Nobody's perfect.

F.MAN: How true. So here goes! (SFX. He throws line out.) Hey, I think I've got a bite!

BERTIE: So fast? But that never happens!

F.MAN: I know! Very odd. And…whoa! Very strong. Help me out here!

A TUG OF WAR ENSUES BACK AND FORTH 3 OR 4 TIMES WITH LOTS OF SFXS. ON THE LAST PULL THERE IS A SOUND AS IN A WHALE BREECHING.

F.MAN: Holy Mackerel! Would you look at that?

BERTIE: I'm looking! I'm looking!

MAGIC: What is all this commotion? Haven't you ever caught a fish before?

F.MAN: Well, yes, I've caught a few…but nothing like you! What are you?

MAGIC: Well, I'm not the little mermaid! I told you…I'm a fish. And I was just leaving to go shopping. (He has a Trader Joe's bag and perhaps an umbrella.)

F.MAN: Oh, sorry. Didn't mean to interrupt, but could you just tell us what KIND of fish you are?

MAGIC: Well, why don't you guess what kind of fish I am? (MUSIC cue) Wait, I'll give you some hints.

SONG #3 I COULDN'T BE AN OCTOPUS

I COULDN'T BE AN OCTOPUS.
I'M SHORT A FEW ARMS.
BUT THEN AGAIN AN OCTOPUS JUST
WOULDN'T HAVE MY CHARMS

SPOKEN:

I couldn't possibly be an octopus. Do I look like an octopus? An octopus has eight arms. I don't have eight arms! Therefore, I am not an octopus!

(SINGS) IF I GAINED A FEW MORE POUNDS,
PERHAPS I'D BE A WHALE.
BUT THEN YOU KNOW I'D HAVE
TO HAVE AN ENORMOUS TAIL!

SPOKEN:

DO I LOOK LIKE A WHALE? No way! Whales have holes on top of their heads. I don't. I got gills, baby!

(SINGS) IF I WERE AN OYSTER,
I'D WEAR THIS ENORMOUS PEARL.

SPOKEN:

Hey, this isn't my pearl! This is an old tire from a car! All the junk people throw in the ocean. No respect I tell you. (He rummages.) Ah, here it is. Beautiful! But I don't think I'm an oyster. If I were, I'd live in a shell. And I don't. So, I'm not an oyster! Simple!

(SINGS) IF I GLOWED IN THE DARK, I'D BE AN ELECTRIC EEL!

SPOKEN:

(**With SFX**) Shocking!

**(SINGS) NO, NO YOU SEE I'M NOT AN OCTOPUS,
NOR WHALE NOR CLAM.
NOR OYSTER, NOR EEL, I AM WHAT I AM
A DENIZEN OF THE SEA, A LOVER OF THE BRINE.
NOW TELL ME WHAT YOU THINK
IS THE NAME I CALL MINE!**

MAGIC: Well, can you guess what I am?

BERTIE: Yes. You're a guppy!

MAGIC: And you're a talking pelican?

BERTIE: Well, YOU'RE a singing fish!

MAGIC: True enough. I guess that makes us even. Anyway, I am not a guppy. Guppies are tiny and I am extra large.

F.MAN: Let me guess. You're an angelfish!

MAGIC: No, although I am heavenly.

F.MAN: A tuna?

MAGIC: I am not a chicken of the sea. You'll never guess, so I'll have to tell you. I am Phil A....Phil A. O'Fish. But my friends call me MAGIC, because I am MAGIC!

BERTIE: You must be joking!

MAGIC: No, I'm not joking, although I'm good at that too. For instance…What time is it when an elephant sits on your fence? Give up? It's time to get a new fence! (He laughs very hard.) But, seriously folks, I grant wishes.

BERTIE: Wishes? You grant wishes? What are you some kind of saltwater Sabu? An underwater genie looking for a lamp? Hmmmm?

MAGIC: No. And don't be such a wise guy! Remember, I am magical. I can turn you into a jellyfish if you're not careful!

BERTIE: Jellyfish, Schmellyfish. I'm not afraid of you!

MAGIC:	Just watch it! Now be quiet please. Fisherman, if you will set me free, I will grant you anything you wish.
F.MAN:	Let me see. No, I can't think of a thing to wish for. Thanks anyway. But I'll still set you free.
MAGIC:	There must be something you could wish for…perhaps a new fishing rod, or a boat, or maybe a less annoying friend to take fishing.
BERTIE:	HEY!
F.MAN:	Nope. Nothing. Here, let me remove this hook so you will be free. (SFX) There you go!
MAGIC:	Thank you, good Fisherman. And remember, if there is anything you wish for, just come to the sea and call me by name. That's MAGIC to you friend…MAGIC FISH. Goodbye now good Fisherman.
F.MAN:	Goodbye Mr. Fish. (SFX) Do you believe it Bertie? A magic fish that grants wishes. Amazing!
BERTIE:	Yeah, but can he do this? (She pirouettes and plies.)
F.MAN:	What was that?
BERTIE:	That was my plié from Swan Lake.
F.MAN:	Oh plie-eze. The fish can't do that. He doesn't have any feet. Come on "show off." Let's go home and tell my wife about the Magic Fish. She'll be so excited.
BERTIE:	She'll be excited all right when she sees you have no fish for dinner and only a "fish tale" to tell!
F.MAN:	We'll see about that.

SCENE CHANGE MUSIC: LITTLE HUT

SCENE 3   THE HUT

F.MAN:	(Entering) Wife! Wife! Wife! I have the most incredible thing to tell you! Wife! Where are you?
WIFE:	(Entering) Back so soon? That was quick. Hand over the catch so I can start dinner.

F.MAN:	No, good wife, I have news. You won't believe what happened!
WIFE:	Tell me…what happened?
F.MAN:	Well, I cast my line into the sea as usual, and after a few seconds I felt a tremendous tug on the line. I thought that surely I had caught the largest flat fish ever. But I was wrong. You'll never guess what I caught!
WIFE:	I can't wait…Tell me!
F.MAN:	It was a MAGIC FISH! You should have seen him. He was all glittery and very nicely dressed for a fish. He said he granted wishes, and if I were to let him go he would give me anything I wished for.
WIFE:	A magic fish?
F.MAN:	Yes.
WIFE:	Who grants wishes.
F.MAN:	Yes.
WIFE:	And nicely dressed.
F.MAN:	Yep.
WIFE:	I see.
F.MAN:	(Nods happily)
WIFE:	Really, good husband. It's bad enough you return without dinner, but making up a story like that…it's just too much.
F.MAN:	But it's true! Please believe me. He really did talk and sing, and…
WIFE:	All right, all right. I believe you. So, what did you wish for?
F.MAN:	What?
WIFE:	Yes, WHAT did you wish for? You must have wished for something! What was it? Perhaps a new dress or some jewelry for your loving wife, hmmmm?
F.MAN:	Nope, nothing. I told him we were quite happy here in our little hut and wished for nothing. So, I removed the hook and set him free.
WIFE:	You did what?

F.MAN: I removed the hook and set him free?

WIFE: You removed the hook and set him free.

F.MAN: Yes, that's exactly what I did.

WIFE: Oh, husband. How could you be so foolish? Here you had someone willing and able to give you anything you wanted and you turned him down? Think, man! There are many things you could have wished for!

F.MAN: Like what? What could I wish for? Tell me, what would YOU wish for?

WIFE: (MUSIC STARTS)
Hmmm. Let me think. What would I wish for?

SONG #4: JUST ONE WISH

**JUST ONE WISH, ONE LITTLE WISH.
I'VE NEVER HAD A WISH BEFORE.
IT COULD BE SO EXCITING,
SOMEONE COMING TO MY DOOR
WITH SOMETHING SPECIAL, SAYING
"HERE'S WHAT YOU WISHED FOR."**

**ONE WISH IS ALL I'M ASKING
ONE WISH IS ALL I'M ASKING FOR.**

**IF YOU HAD A WISH WHAT WOULD YOU WISH FOR?
A PUPPY OR A KITTEN WOULD BE NICE.
A TREE TO CLIMB, A SWING TO SWING,
IT COULD BE SO MANY THINGS,
IF YOU HAD A WISH, WHAT WOULD IT BE?**

JUST ONE WISH, ETC. (Wife can interact with the audience)

**ONE LITTLE WISH IS ALL I'M ASKING.
JUST ONE WISH, ONE LITTLE WISH.
I NEVER HAD A WISH BEFORE!**

F.MAN: Well, we don't need a puppy, or a kitten. We have a perfectly good tree, and I can make us a swing. So, I guess I still have nothing to wish for.

WIFE: How about a new house to live in? Wouldn't it be nice to live in a nice little cottage instead of this dump we call home?

F.MAN: Dump?

WIFE: Dump.

F.MAN: Gee, we've always been happy in this dump.

WIFE: I know. But just think of it. A beautiful little cottage, yellow perhaps, with window boxes full of pretty red flowers and covered in aluminum siding so you wouldn't have to paint it every year, hmmmm?

F.MAN: It does sound nice.

WIFE: Doesn't it? Now go to your fish and get our wish. Remember, yellow cottage, flower boxes, red flowers, aluminum siding and, oh, tell him the curtains should be blue.

F.MAN: I'm on my way. Come on, Bertie, let's go.

WIFE: (Singing like a child.) I'm getting a new house, I'm getting a new house!

LIGHTS FADE: UP AGAIN ON OCEAN

SCENE 5: THE OCEAN

F.MAN: Yellow cottage, red flowers, blue curtains (He repeats this phrase several times) Ah, here we are Bertie. This is where we saw THE MAGIC FISH!

BERTIE: Hmmm. Clouds in the sky, choppy water, rising barometric pressure. Perfect conditions for a gathering storm at the favorite seaside fishing spot.

F.MAN: Are you practicing to be a weather forecaster?

BERTIE: Just trying to help.

F.MAN: Well, thanks, but I need to call the fish now. Stand back.

**MAGIC FISH, OH MAGIC FISH
COME TO ME NOW FOR I HAVE A WISH!**

SFX. THE FISH APPEARS IN A SHOWER CAP WITH A BATH BRUSH AND A RUBBER DUCKIE.

MAGIC: Hellooo, Fisherman. I'm afraid you caught us in the shower, my little rubber duckie and I. (SFX Quack, quack) Oooh, it's a little chilly up here. We have to get back to our nice hot shower…so, what can I do for you?

F.MAN: Well, I was thinking it over and…

MAGIC: Yes…

F.MAN: And, although I said before there was nothing I wanted to wish for…

MAGIC: Yes…

F.MAN: Well, there is something that I want after all.

MAGIC: Yes…there always is. Well, hurry up and make your wish. I'm freezing my scales off up here!

F.MAN: I wish for a nice little cottage to replace our hut. It should be…(tentatively) yellow, with flower boxes, red flowers, aluminum siding…and, oh yes, blue curtains.

MAGIC: Yellow, red and blue…Hmmmm nice primary colors. Well, you shall get your wish. Now stand back. Sometimes this gets messy.

(SFX under chant)

IKKETY AKETTY OOOH!
BIKETY BAKETY BOO!
EEK EH EH
OIK AH AH
GINK!

Go home, Fisherman. There is now a cottage where your hut used to stand.

F.MAN: Thank you great Fish! You have made us very happy!

MAGIC: Yeah, yeah, yeah. (Duck Quacks.) Okay, Duckie, we're going. (Quacks again.) Okay, Okay! I said we're going…Watch your manners. I really do have to go now, Fisherman. Goodbye!

SFX

F.MAN: Come on, Bertie, let's go see our new home!

BERTIE: Do you think maybe there will be a new pie too?

F.MAN: Maybe.

MUSIC SCENE CHANGE

SCENE 6
LOVELY COTTAGE WITH ALL THE PRIMARY COLOR FEATURES REQUESTED

F.MAN: Wife! Wife! Oh, Bert, look! The cottage! It's exactly what she asked for!

BERTIE: It certainly is yellow. Let's see if there's a…HEY< NO PIE! What's going on?

WIFE: (Entering) Oh, good husband, isn't it beautiful? Just what I wanted. And a nice big kitchen with a new oven to bake my pies. It even has a cooling rack so I don't have to set them on the window sill anymore!

BERTIE: RATS!

WIFE: What was that, Husband?

F.MAN: What was what?

WIFE: (She looks confused for a moment, then shakes her head). Oh, never mind. Just look at this place. This is the cottage I've dreamed of!

F.MAN: Good. I like it too. You were right. It is better than living in the old hut. I'm glad I went to the fish and asked him for this cottage. And just think, I'll never have to paint it! We'll be happy here for the rest of our lives!

WIFE: Yeeeesss, but.

F.MAN: What?

WIFE: If the fish could get us this cottage, couldn't he give us something better?

F.MAN: Better?

WIFE: Yes, better. Like…a MANSION!

F.MAN: WHAT?!

WIFE: Yes, a beautiful mansion…like in "GONE WITH THE WIND." It must have columns and porches, and great big windows that you can walk through. Oh, and servants. I must have maids and a butler, and a cook. Of course I'll teach the cook how to bake my pies. And I must have beautiful gowns and jewelry to match and…

F.MAN: Wait a minute. We can't do that! Look, this cottage is great. There's only the two of us..and the pelican. Why would we need a huge mansion?

WIFE: The point isn't that we need it. It's that we can GET it. Now, go to your fish and get my wish!

F.MAN: But…

WIFE: But nothing! What is so hard about this? Don't be a foolish man! Just go! (She exits abruptly.)

BERTIE: Whoa. I never heard her talk to you like that before. "Foolish man?" What's happening?

F.MAN: I'm not sure I know.

MUSIC STARTS: LIGHT CHANGE

SONG #5: GOOD HUSBAND

SHE USED TO CALL ME "GOOD HUSBAND."
I WAS THE APPLE OF HER EYE.
SHE USED TO KNOW WHEN I WAS HAPPY
AND WHEN I WAS ABOUT TO CRY.

NOW IT DOESN'T SEEM TO MATTER.
NOW SHE CALLS ME "FOOLISH MAN."
WHATEVER HAPPENED TO ALL THE LAUGHTER
IN OUR HOUSE WHERE IT ALL BEGAN?

MUST I STAND ASIDE AND SEE
ALL THESE THINGS HAPPENING?
IS THERE NOTHING I CAN DO
TO FIND THE LIFE THAT WE ONCE KNEW?

SHE USED TO CALL ME "GOOD HUSBAND."
I WAS THE APPLE OF HER EYE.
SHE USED TO KNOW WHEN I WAS HAPPY,
AND WHEN I WAS ABOUT TO CRY.

Come on, Bertie, Let's go.

LIGHTS DIM, MUSIC SEGUE. OCEAN STORM SOUNDS.

SCENE 7   THE STORMY OCEAN

F.MAN: Well, here we are.

BERTIE: Wow, look at that water. It's really rough. A storm is definitely on the way. (THUNDER SFX) Ooooo, thunder too! Let's make this quick, okay? I don't want to get caught in the rain. You know how I hate the smell of wet feathers…even my own!

F.MAN: I hope the fish can hear me over all the noise!

**MAGIC FISH, OH MAGIC FISH,
COME TO ME NOW, FOR I HAVE A WISH!**

SFX FISH APPEARS

MAGIC: Ho there, Fisherman! What are you doing out in this weather? (SFX Telephone) Oops, there's my phone. Hold on a sec, wouldya while I get this call? (He pulls out his cell phone) Hello, hello! What? What? I can't hear you. Naw, no thanks, I don't need flood insurance. Gotta go now. (He ends call, puts phone away.) So, Fisherman, how are ya'? What can I do for you?

F.MAN: Well, it seems my wife is not happy with the cottage.

MAGIC: No?

F.MAN: No.

MAGIC: Oh. Well, I can give you back your hut if you like. That's always an option.

F.MAN: No, that won't work. You see, she wants something a little larger. Have you anything in the way of a…mansion?

MAGIC: She wants a mansion.

F.MAN: Yes. (cringing as if expecting the Fish to explode) And a full staff of servants for her to order about. And…gowns and jewelry to go with it.

MAGIC: Gowns and jewelry, eh?

F.MAN: (Still cringing) Yes.

MAGIC: Well, I will try my best.

IKKETY AKETY OOOH!
BIKETY BAKETTY BOO!
EEK EH EH
OIK AH AH
GINK!

Done! She has her mansion with all the trimmings. Now go home, Fisherman. The storm is coming. And make sure you get that bird inside. The smell of wet feathers! YUCK. I gotta go now…pressing business…gotta do my ironing! See ya! (SFX)

F.MAN: Let's go Bertie. Let's see if my wife is happy with the mansion.

BERTIE: You know, that fish tells the worst jokes…pressing business…ironing. Man!

F.MAN: I know, he's not a very good comedian…but, he does grant wishes. If that can keep my wife happy, that's enough for me. Let's go home.

MUSIC SEGUE: JUST ONE WISH. OCEAN NOISE FADES.

SCENE 8   A MANSION

MUSIC CHANGES TO #6 "MINOR MASTERPIECE THEME."

WIFE: (Talking to "servants" offstage with a pseudo-cultured accent) Remember, Hilda, only one cup of sugar in that pie. If you make it too sweet I shall have to dismiss you and find another cook. Beatrice, dear, make sure you dust all the crystals in the chandeliers, and, for heaven's sake, Horace, can't you DO something about the bees in the honeysuckle? HOW am I supposed to sit in the garden?

F.MAN: (Entering with Bertie) Wow! The mansion! It's huge! It must have a hundred rooms!

WIFE: Only fifty. What would we DO with a hundred rooms? (She laughs) But it does have marble staircases, and crystal chandeliers, and a magnificent art gallery. And guess what…we now own the Mona Lisa and Whistler's Mother!

F.MAN: What?! But that's not right! We can't OWN other people!

WIFE: (Laughing) Don't be silly. They're paintings, not people. Oh good husband, we will really be happy here.

F.MAN: You think so? I see you have your gowns and jewelry. What about servants?

WIFE: We have plenty. You're not going to have to do a thing around here.

F.MAN: That's going to be weird. I've always done things for myself.

WIFE: Then this will be a refreshing change. What about all those things you don't like doing—like painting the door, for instance—get it?

F.MAN: Hmmmm. Painting the door you say?

WIFE: Yes, and painting the house…

F.MAN: (Getting into the idea.) And painting the house. Right!

WIFE: And having to go fishing every day.

F.MAN: Fishing…I like fishing.

WIFE: Well, then you could still do that. AND you could do it whenever you wanted to!

F.MAN: Hmmm. Maybe I COULD get used to living like this.

WIFE: Of course you could. We're living in the lap of luxury now. Did you notice there is a little mansion out back for the pelican to live in? It looks just like ours, except she doesn't have servants, of course.

BERTIE: RATS!

WIFE: What was that, Husband?

F.MAN: What was what?

WIFE: (Again confused.) Oh, never mind. Shall we go inside? This mansion is truly a "palace." WAIT A MINUTE! Good Husband, I just hatched the most wonderful idea! Guess what I'm thinking!

F.MAN: (To Bertie) She just called me "Good Husband." I like that! (To WIFE) Tell me good wife, what is your wonderful idea?

WIFE: I'll give you a clue. I just said this mansion is like a "palace." (Speaking very distinctly) A "pal-ace." Get it?

F.MAN: A "pal-ace." A palace. Oooh, A "palace"…like a "Cas-**tle**."

WIFE: I think you've got the idea!

F.MAN: As in, "What could be better than a mansion?" A "Cas-**tle**" of course!

WIFE: Of course!

F.MAN:	Of course! I could have thought of that. I could go ask the fish for a CAS-TLE!
WIFE:	Yes! A CAS-TLE!
F.MAN:	I think I'm getting the hang of this! And you know what else, Wife?
WIFE:	What, Good Husband?
F.MAN:	If we are going to LIVE like royalty, we might as well BE royalty!
WIFE:	(Coyly) Why, whatever are you thinking, Good Husband?
F.MAN:	Well, I'll go to the fish and ask him for a castle. THEN I will tell him to make us King and Queen!
WIFE:	Excellent! I'll go with you! (Singing) I'M GOING TO BE QUEEN, I'M GOING TO BE QUEEN!
F.MAN:	(Singing) I'M GOING TO BE KING! I'M GOING TO BE KING!
	(They exit singing, voices fading)
BERTIE:	(Singing to herself) I'm going to stay here. I'm going to stay here. (Speaking) Boy, this smells like trouble to me!

BLACK OUT
OCEAN SOUNDS

SCENE 9   AN EVEN STORMIER OCEAN

LIGHTS UP

WIFE:	Wow. Look at those waves!
F.MAN:	Even without my weatherbird, I can tell the storm is coming.
WIFE:	Without your what?
F.MAN:	Oh, never mind. Let's make this quick. The wind is so loud I'm afraid the fish won't hear me. I know. Let's call him together.
WIFE:	Okay. How?
F.MAN:	Repeat after me: **MAGIC FISH, OH MAGIC FISH**

WIFE:	**MAGIC FISH, OH MAGIC FISH.**
F.MAN:	Good. **COME TO ME NOW, FOR I HAVE A WISH!**
WIFE:	**GOOD. COME TO ME NOW FOR I HAVE A WISH!**
F.MAN:	That was great. Only don't say "good." Are you ready?
WIFE:	Yes, I am. Let's become King and Queen!
F.MAN:	Okay. When I count to three we'll call him. One, Two, Three…
BOTH:	**MAGIC FISH, OH MAGIC FISH.** **COME TO ME NOW, FOR I HAVE A WISH!**

SFX: FISH APPEARS

MAGIC:	Hello there! Whoa! Look at that sky. I have to get my raincoat and umbrella. Be right back. (SFX UP AND DOWN) There, that's better. Hello again, Fisherman. And hello to you, Mrs.Fisherman.
WIFE:	Nice to meet you.
MAGIC:	What's the occasion?
F.MAN:	Well, the mansion is beautiful.
MAGIC:	I aim to please.
F.MAN:	But…we figured if we're going to live like royalty, we might as well BE royalty. Therefore, we wish to be King and Queen.
MAGIC:	You do.
WIFE:	And to live in a castle.
MAGIC:	But of course. Where else would you live? Okay, here goes. **IKKETY AKETY, OOOOH!** **BIKETY, BAKETY, BOO!** **EEK EH EH** **OIK AH AH** **GINK!** Go home to your castle. You are now King and Queen.

F.MAN:	Thank you, MAGIC FISH. This will satisfy us and we will be content.
MAGIC:	Hah! I'm not gonna bet the farm on it. Now look, the storm is here. Go home quickly and be careful. I'm going back inside for some hot tomato soup and a grilled cheese sandwich. See ya!

SFX

F.MAN:	Shall we go see our palace?
WIFE:	Yes, Your Highness!

OCEAN SOUNDS UP THEN FADE. LIGHTS FADE. SONG #7 ROYAL MUSIC

SCENE 10   A CASTLE. BERTIE IS ON STAGE

BERTIE:	I hear royal music. I guess that means they did it! Oh, brother. Here they come.
WIFE:	Oh look, it's the pelican. Excuse me, Pelican. You're supposed to bow in front of your King and Queen. (Bertie awkwardly bows.) That's better. Now, I am going inside to make sure that everyone is doing what they are supposed to be doing. Good Husband…I mean, my King, would you see to it that the drawbridge is raised?
F.MAN:	Yes, my Queen. Anon, Alas, and alack. Forsooth and Forthwith. (She exits.)
	Now…as for you, lowly Pelican. I know we were friends in the past, but now I am King, and you are merely a bird. Surely you understand that we can no longer pal around like we used to. And, by the way, there will be no more pies. You cannot expect the Queen to bake pies, can you?
BERTIE:	Holy Cow!
F.MAN:	What did you say?
BERTIE:	I said, "Holy Cow!"
F.MAN:	"Holy Cow"…..what?
BERTIE:	Holy Cow, I can't believe what you said, and that you're dumping me as a friend after all the time we've spent together.

F.MAN: Holy Cow, I can't believe what you said, and that you're dumping me as a friend after all the time we've spent together…what?

BERTIE: (Seeing the light) Oh, I get it…Holy Cow, etcetera, etcetera, "Your Majesty."

F.MAN: That's better. Now bow. (She does) Good. Now grovel. (She does) Very nice. I do love to make others bow and grovel. It is so much fun. Don't you agree?

BERTIE: Yes, Your Majesty.

ROYAL MUSIC: QUEEN ENTERS

F.MAN: Ah, my Queen.

WIFE: Ah, my King. You will never guess what I have just done.

F.MAN: I tingle with anticipation, my Queen.

WIFE: I have just decreed that a ball be held in honor of us. I have ordered everyone in the kingdom to attend and each must bring the most valuable thing they own to present to us as a gift. Doesn't that sound like a good time?

F.MAN: Indeed it does sound jolly. Now, Milady I am feeling kingly hunger pangs. Shall we go in and have the servants scare up a couple of royal peanut butter and jelly sandwiches?

WIFE: Indeed we shall, Your Hungry Highness.

F.MAN: After you, my Majesty.

THEY EXIT LAUGHING

BERTIE: Boy, this has really gotten out of hand. And on top of everything, I've lost a friend.

SONG #8. WHAT DO YOU DO?

**WHAT DO YOU DO WHEN A FRIENDSHIP IS THROUGH,
DO YOU CRY YOUR EYES OUT?
WHAT DO YOU DO WHEN YOU FEEL SO BLUE?**

**AND HOW DO YOU KNOW WHEN IT'S TIME TO GO,
DO YOU HEAR A CLOCK CHIME?
AND WHERE DOES IT SAY THAT YOU'VE GOT TO STAY
WHERE YOU'RE NOT WANTED?**

> **WHY DOES IT SEEM LIKE THIS IS A DREAM
> AND I WISH I'D WAKE UP?**
>
> **WHAT DO YOU DO WHEN A FRIENDSHIP IS THROUGH,
> DO YOU CRY YOUR EYES OUT?
> WHAT DO YOU DO WHEN YOU FEEL SO BLUE?**
>
> **AND HOW CAN IT BE THAT I FAIL TO SEE THE
> WHY OR WHERE FOR?
> AND IS IT ALL RIGHT TO SEE THE LIGHT
> AND JUST WALK AWAY?**
>
> **WHY DOES IT SEEM LIKE THIS IS A DREAM
> AND I WISH I'D WAKE UP?**
>
> **WHAT DO YOU DO WHEN A FRIENDSHIP IS THROUGH?
> DO YOU CRY YOUR EYES OUT?
> WHAT DO YOU DO? WHAT DO YOU?**

SONG MUSIC SEGUES INTO ROYAL MUSIC

BERTIE: (Speaking) Oh, oh. Here they come.

WIFE: (Entering with the King) That certainly was a fine lunch, wasn't it?

F.MAN: It certainly was. I don't think I have ever had a finer sandwich. It surely was fun when you were ordering the cook around! Then…when she slipped and almost fell… (He laughs) That was hilarious. I do think you make her a little nervous.

WIFE: So what if I do. She is there for me to order around. I do love to order people around. Order, order, order.

F.MAN: I know what you mean. Such a sense of power!

BERTIE: Oh, brother!

THE FISHERMAN AND WIFE IGNORE HIM.

WIFE: But tell me the truth, Kingly King, don't you wish you had even more power? I know I do.

F.MAN: Yes, but we are already the King and Queen. We can't get any more powerful than that.

WIFE: Oooo my Kingy Poo. I have an idea!

F.MAN: Why, my Queensy—whatever could it be this time?

WIFE: What if—what if we were able to control the Sun and the Moon? That would make us more powerful.

F.MAN: (Dropping his kingly demeanor.) Oooo. I don't think that's possible!

WIFE: Nonsense! Anything is possible. When you woke up this morning did you think you would be King before lunchtime?

F.MAN: No.

WIFE: And did you think we would possess this glorious castle?

F.MAN: No.

WIFE: And did you think…..?

F.MAN: No. I mean, okay, okay, I get it!

WIFE: I'm glad you agree. Now, would you rather have the Sun…or the Moon?

F.MAN: I believe I'll choose the Sun.

WIFE: Perfect. Then I shall control the Moon!

BERTIE: Oh BROTHER!

WIFE: Who keeps saying, "Oh BROTHER?"

BERTIE: That would be me. "Oh BROTHER!"

F.MAN: Now, what is your problem, lowly Pelican? And make it quick. I'm off to see the MAGIC FISH. The Queen and I are going to have power over the Sun and the Moon!

BERTIE: That sounds very dangerous to me, Your Highness!

F.MAN: I am the KING! I laugh at danger! (He laughs.)

WIFE: That's my King!

BERTIE: Bur aren't you two happy being King and Queen?

F.MAN: Of course, but don't you see? We can be so much MORE powerful!

WIFE:	That's right. With the King controlling the Sun and me controlling the Moon, we'll be able to control the Universe!
BERTIE:	You're both OUT of control. This isn't right!
F.MAN:	Out of my way puny Pelican! I know what I want and I get what I want!
WIFE:	That's my King! Now, go to the fish and get our wish! And you, Ms. Talking Pelican, go away before I order the cook to make Pelican Pizza!

SHE EXITS INTO CASTLE. FISHERMAN EXITS TO THE OCEAN

BERTIE:	Oh Brother. Now neither of them will listen to me.

BLACK OUT

SCENE 11   OCEAN ROARING AND STORM RAGING

F.MAN:	**MAGIC FISH, OH MAGIC FISH** **COME TO ME NOW, FOR I HAVE A WISH!**

SFX

MAGIC:	You must be out of your mind coming out in this storm!
F.MAN:	But I have a wish.
MAGIC:	What could you possibly want? You are already King.
F.MAN:	I am. I am King, and my wife, you know, the Queen.
MAGIC:	Yes, I know the Queen.
F.MAN:	Well, the Queen and I want more power.
MAGIC:	Impossible!
F.MAN:	Well, guess what? We want power over the Sun and Moon!
MAGIC:	What? NO ONE may control the Sun and the Moon!
F.MAN:	Yes they can and we will! Now, as your KING, I order you to grant our wish!
MAGIC:	As my King, huh? Well, you don't know what you're getting into. I shall grant you this wish. Then I shall grant you NO MORE! You have made me very angry,

Fisherman King! But I shall let you see for yourself that no man or woman should ever have such power!

F.MAN: Enough! GIVE ME MY WISH NOW!

MAGIC: **SHARKS THAT SWIM BATS THAT FLY,
COMETS RACING CROSS THE SKY.
STARS AND PLANETS HEAR MY CALL.
ONE WISH LEFT AND THAT IS ALL.
THIS MAN AND WIFE,
THEIR WILL BE DONE,
SHALL NOW CONTROL THE MOON AND SUN!**

STORM NOISE RAGES/CURTAIN CLOSES: COMPLETE BLACKOUT/ BLACK LIGHT COMES UP

ON STAGE WE SEE AN IRIDESCENT MOON THE WIFE IS HOLDING

F.MAN: (From offstage) Wife, Wife! I mean Queen, Queen!

WIFE: Here I am Kingly King! And look what I have!

F.MAN: (Entering with sun also iridescent) How magnificent! And look what I have!

BERTIE: (Entering) Your Majesties! Please be careful. This just isn't right.

F.MAN: Stupid bird. The Queen and I will decide what is right. We need no advice from you.

BERTIE: Remember the Fish's warning. Too much power can be dangerous.

WIFE: Nonsense. Now buzz off. Bye bye, Bertie.

BERTIE: All right. I'll go.

F.MAN: I wonder if we can make the sun and moon rise at our command. Shall we try?

WIFE: Yes, you first.

F.MAN: Sun Rise. (The sun rises) Sun set. (The sun sets.) Now, your turn.

WIFE: Moon rise. (The moon rises) Now moon set. (The moon sets.) Oooo that was fun. Now I wonder if we can make them dance. Shall we try?

F.MAN: Yes!

BOTH:	Sun and Moon…DANCE!

SONG #9: INSTRUMENTAL

THEY DANCE TO MUSIC. MUSIC CHANGES TO FIGHTING MUSIC. THE SUN AND MOON BEGIN TO FIGHT. STROBE LIGHT/BLACKLIGHT ETC.

F.MAN:	Oh no, they are fighting!
WIFE:	What should we do?
F.MAN:	We simply need to command them to stop.
BOTH:	STOP FIGHTING SUN AND MOON!
WIFE:	MOON STOP!
F.MAN:	SUN STOP!

MUSIC GETS LOUDER AND LOUDER UNTIL IT SUDDENLY STOPS. COMPLETE BLACKOUT. SUN AND MOON DISAPPEAR.
SFX BLACK HOLE SOUND. (REVERSE GATE)

WIFE:	Good Husband, where are you? I can't see anything. It's pitch black!
F.MAN:	I hear you, Wife, but I can't find you. It's so dark!
WIFE:	Oh Husband, I'm scared.
F.MAN:	So am I. (They bump into each other. Each lights their flashlight on the other.) Oh, here you are. Thank goodness.
WIFE:	What has happened?
F.MAN:	It seems the whole world has disappeared. The fish warned us that something bad could happen. Now what are we going to do?

THE ACTORS CAN GO INTO THE AUDIENCE SHINING THEIR FLASHLIGHTS ON CHILDREN TO ASK THEM WHAT THEY SHOULD DO. BACK UP ON STAGE

WIFE:	I know. You must call the fish again and ask for another wish.
F.MAN:	I can't do that! He said he wouldn't grant any more wishes.
WIFE:	Surely if you explain the situation, he will help us out.

F.MAN: No, he won't. It won't do any good. I won't do it!

WIFE: Then I will!

**MAGIC FISH, OH MAGIC FISH
COME TO ME NOW, FOR I HAVE A WISH!**

MAGIC: (SFX) NO!!! I WARNED YOU, DIDN'T I? YOU HAVE GONE TOO FAR! NO MORE WISHES!

WIFE: Oh great fish, please listen!

SONG #10: THE DAY WAS NIGHT

**THE DAY WAS NIGHT AND THE NIGHT WAS DAY,
THE STARS WERE MOVING EVERY WHICH WAY.
THE DAY WAS SHORT AND THE NIGHT WAS LONG,
I JUST DON'T KNOW WHAT COULD'VE GONE WRONG.**

**THE BIRDS COULDN'T FIND THE MORNING TO SING
AND THE OWL WAS HIDING UNDER HIS WING.
THE NIGHTCRAWLERS CRAWLED IN THE LIGHT OF DAY,
I DON'T KNOW HOW I MADE THINGS THAT WAY.
WHAT A TERRIBLE WAY TO END THE DAY.**

F.MAN: (Entering)
**WE WANTED THE MOON AND WE WANTED THE STARS,
DO YOU THINK MAYBE WE'VE GONE TOO FAR?
I WAS KING AND WHAT DID IT BRING?
I HAD TO HAVE A LITTLE OF EVERYTHING
SO NOW WE COME A BEGGING.**

BOTH: **OH LET US GO BACK TO THE HOUSE BY THE SEA,
WHERE THE KING WAS KING AND WE WERE WE.
WHEN WE PRETTY MUCH KNEW WHAT WOULD HAPPEN NEXT
WHEN THE MOON WOULD RISE AND THE SUN WOULD SET.**

**OH LET US GO BACK TO THE HOUSE BY THE SEA
WHERE WE CAN LIVE EVER HAPPILY.**

MAGIC: **IT COULD POSSIBLY BE ARRANGED I THINK
IF YOU WOULD SIMPLY TAKE THIS DRINK
I'VE PREPARED FOR YOU A MAGIC BREW**

WHICH VERY WELL COULD ALLOW YOU TO GO HOME.

**OH LET THEM GO BACK TO THEIR HOUSE BY THE SEA,
WHERE THERE WAS NO KING, AND I WAS FREE.
WHEN THEY PRETTY MUCH KNEW WHAT WOULD HAPPEN
NEXT WHEN THE MOON WOULD RISE AND THE SUN WOULD SET.**

**OH LET THEM GO BACK TO THE HOUSE BY THE SEA,
WHERE THEY CAN LIVE EVER HAPPILY.**

SFX: RUMBLES / CURTAIN OPENS/ MUSIC: DVORAK'S LARGO #11

LIGHTS UP

SCENE 12
THE ORIGINAL LITTLE HUT. PELICAN IS SITTING ON THE PILING

WIFE: Oh, Good Husband, look! Our beautiful little hut! We're back home!

F.MAN: Yes, we're back! And look, here's Bertie! Hey Bertie!

WIFE: Oh, am I ever glad to see you, you pretty Pelican!

BERTIE: (Bertie looks around confused. Indicates himself.) Pretty Pelican? Me? You're calling me a pretty Pelican?

F.MAN: (Calling offstage) Thank you Magic Fish. Everything's back to normal…kind of.

MAGIC: (Walks on stage) You're very welcome. You know, it's a very cute hut. But here's a thought. If you ever decide you want something bigger, why don't you just build it and save us all a whole lot of trouble.

WIFE: We never thought of that! What a great idea!

F.MAN: Well, Good Wife, do you think we can be happy now?

WIFE: I suppose. BUT…

All: Oh NO!

WIFE: I think we need…a PIE! No, make that two pies. One for us and one for my pretty little pelican!

BERTIE: My very own pie.

SONG #12

ALL: **IN A LITTLE HUT BY THE SEA
WHERE WE LIVE, YOU AND ME
IT ISN'T MUCH, BUT WE'RE HAPPY
HERE IN OUR LITTLE HUT BY THE SEA!**

BLACK OUT

**FINALE: BOWS
SONG #13, THE SEA CAN BE MAGIC**

BERTIE: **IF EVER YOU COME ACROSS A FISH AND THINK YOU MIGHT LIKE A WISH
REMEMBER THE STORY WE JUST TOLD,
EVEN WHEN YOU'RE OLD.**

MAGIC: **YOU CAN WISH ON A STAR OR WISH ON ME,
IT REALLY DOESN'T MATTER YOU SEE.
THE WORLD IS FULL OF MAGIC THINGS
CRYSTAL BALLS, ENCHANTED RINGS.**

ALL: **THE SEA CAN BE MAGIC, BUT SO ARE YOU.
THE BEST WISH IS THE ONE YOU YOURSELF
MAKE COME TRUE.
THE SEA CAN BE MAGIC, BUT SO ARE YOU.
THE BEST WISH IS THE ONE YOU YOURSELF
MAKE COME TRUE!**

MUSIC FROM
THE MAGIC FISH

A One-Act
Musical for Children

Cover Art by Christine Boyka Kluge

Script by Jan Callner & Bill Wheeler
Music & Lyrics by Jan Callner

Copyright 1998, 2014, 2025
Jan Callner
Mike and Me Productions

Songs:

#1 A Pel-I-Can	The Pelican (Bert/Bertie)
#2 Little Hut by the Sea	Fisherman/Wife
#3 I Couldn't Be an Octopus	The Fish
#4 Just One Wish	The Wife
#5 Good Husband	The Fisherman
#6 Minor Masterpiece	Instrumental
#7 Royal Music	Instrumental
#8a What Do You Do?	Bert/Bertie
#8b What Do You Do? Db	
#9 Sun and Moon Dance/Confusion	Instrumental
#10 The Day Was Night	Fisherman/Wife/Fish
#11 Dvorak's Largo	Instrumental
#12 Little Hut Reprise	Fisherman/Wife/Bert(ie)
#13 The Sea Can Be Magic	All

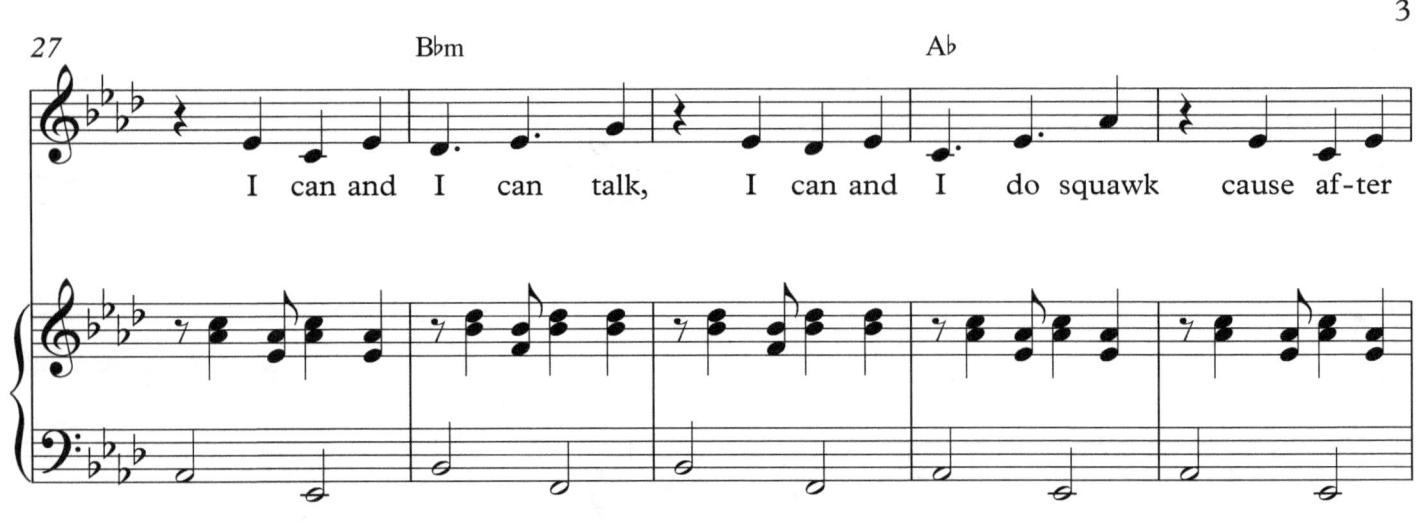

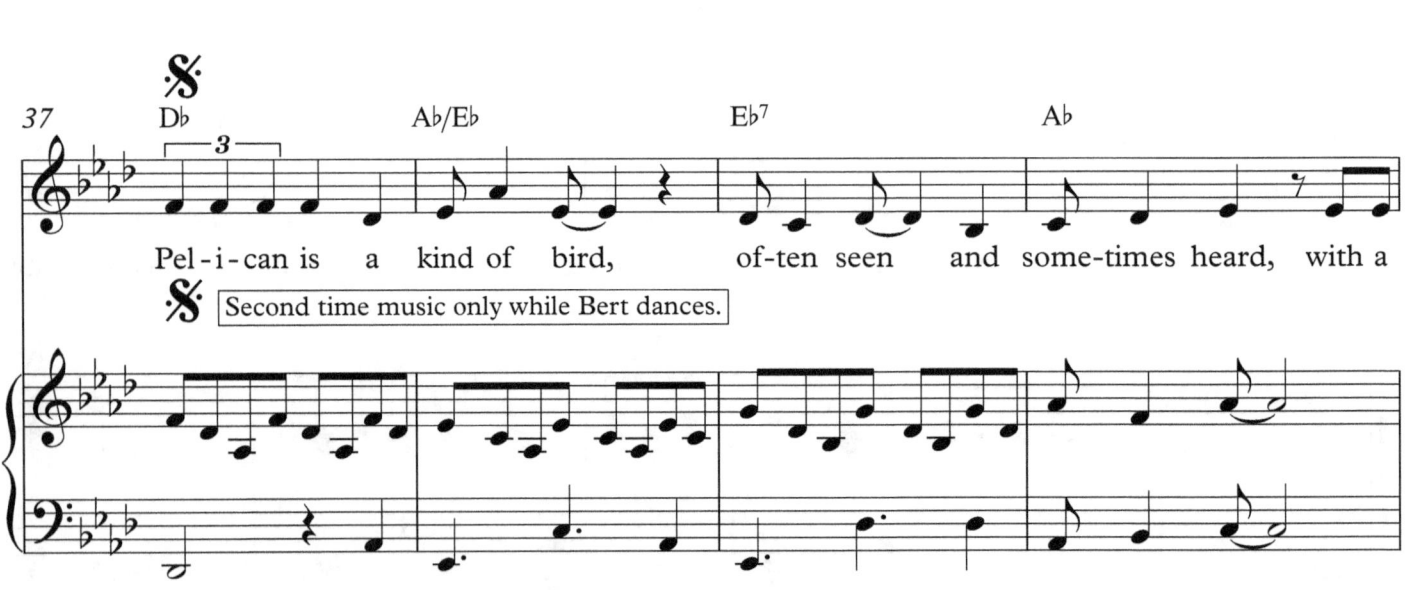

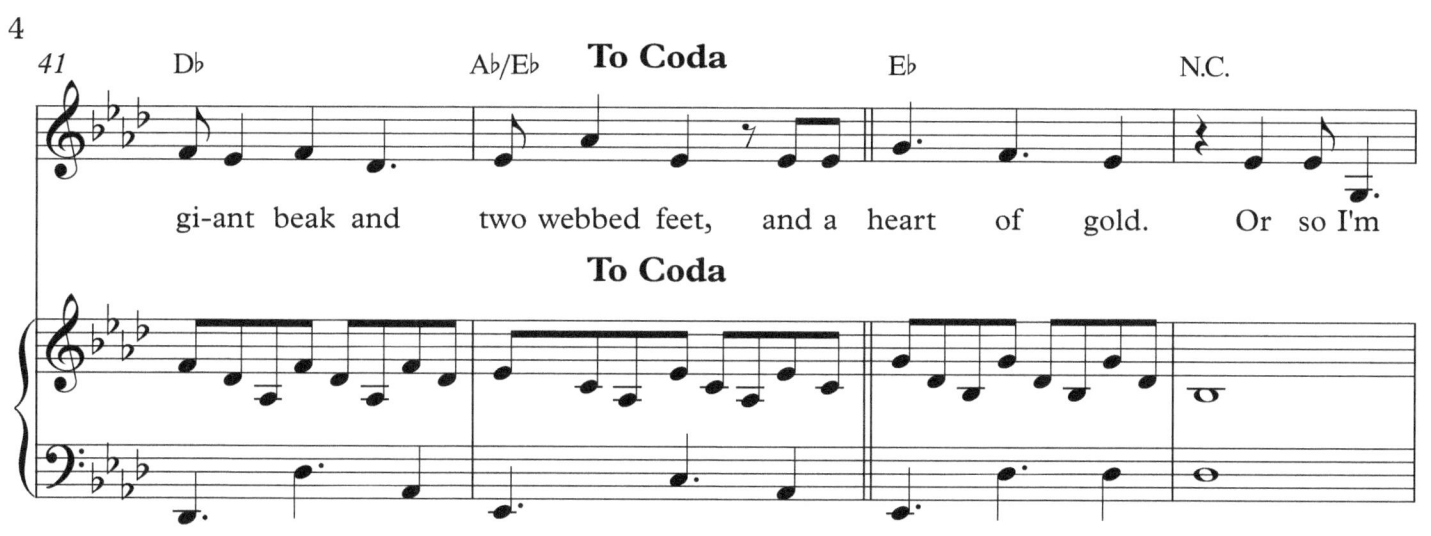
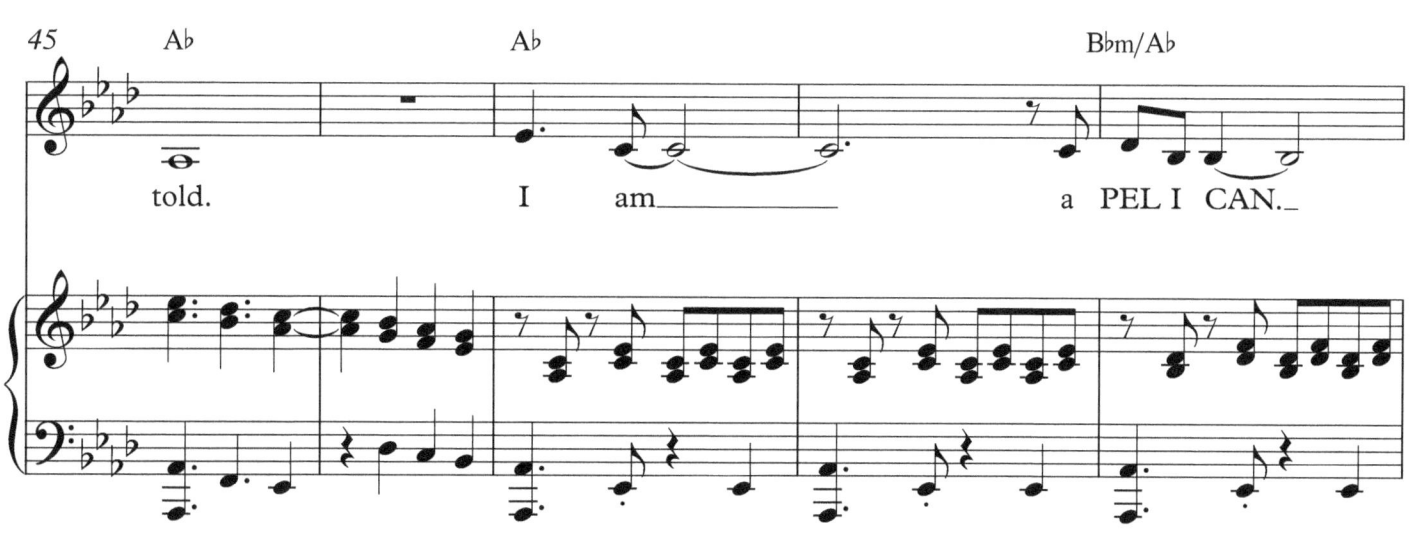

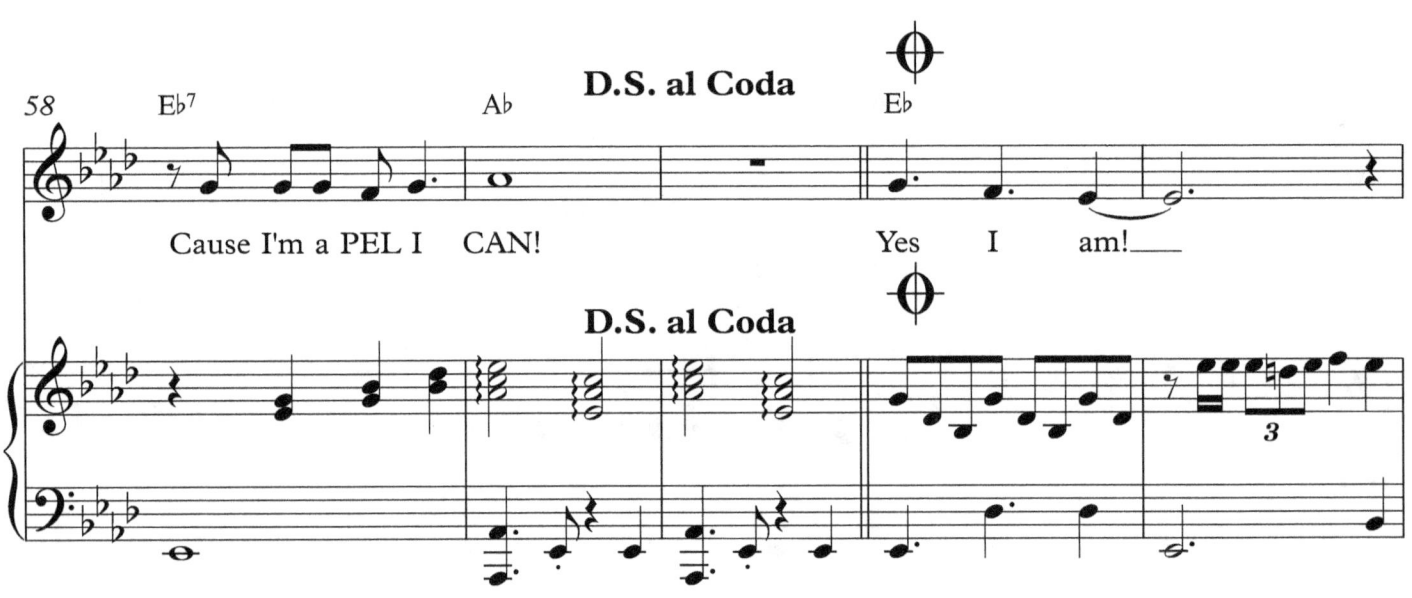

Little Hut by the Sea

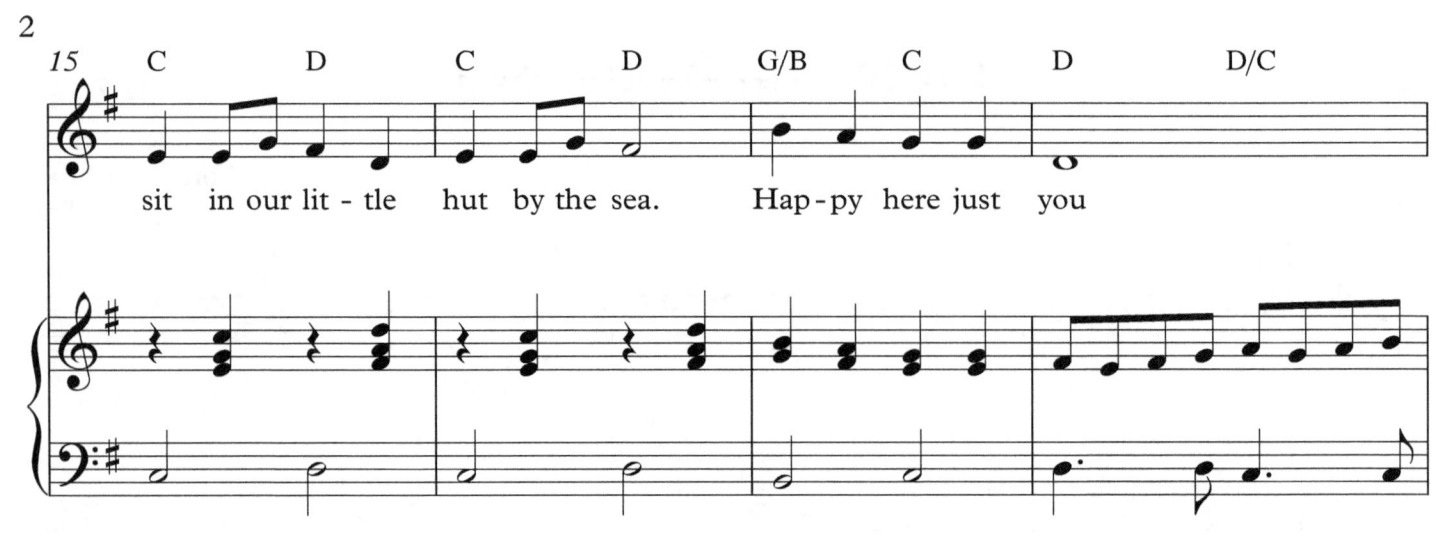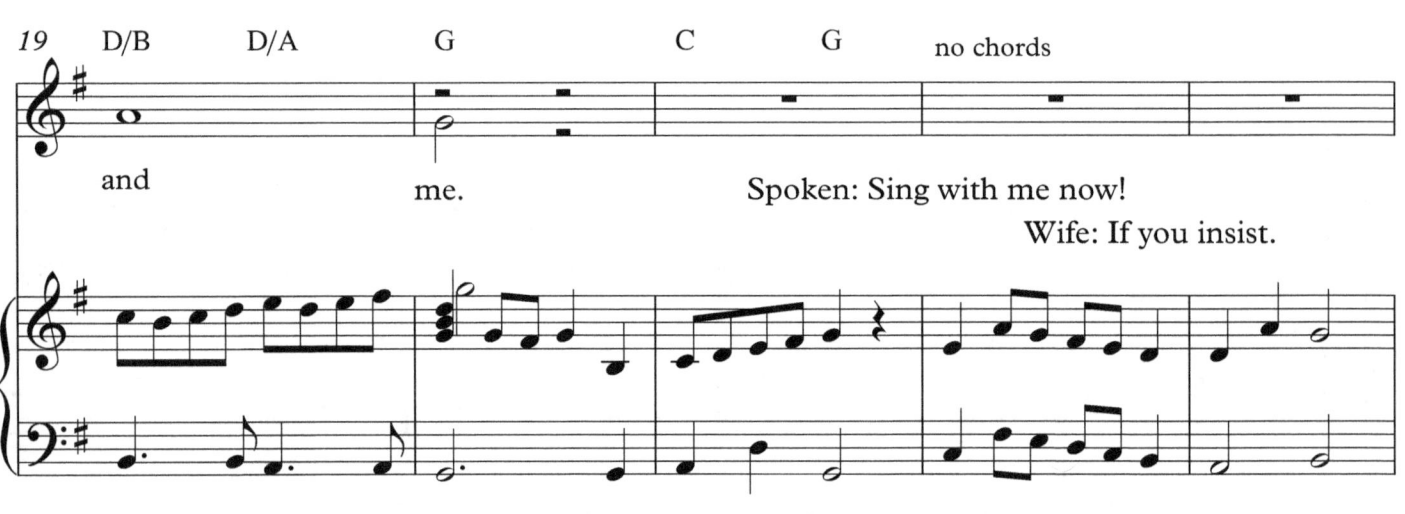

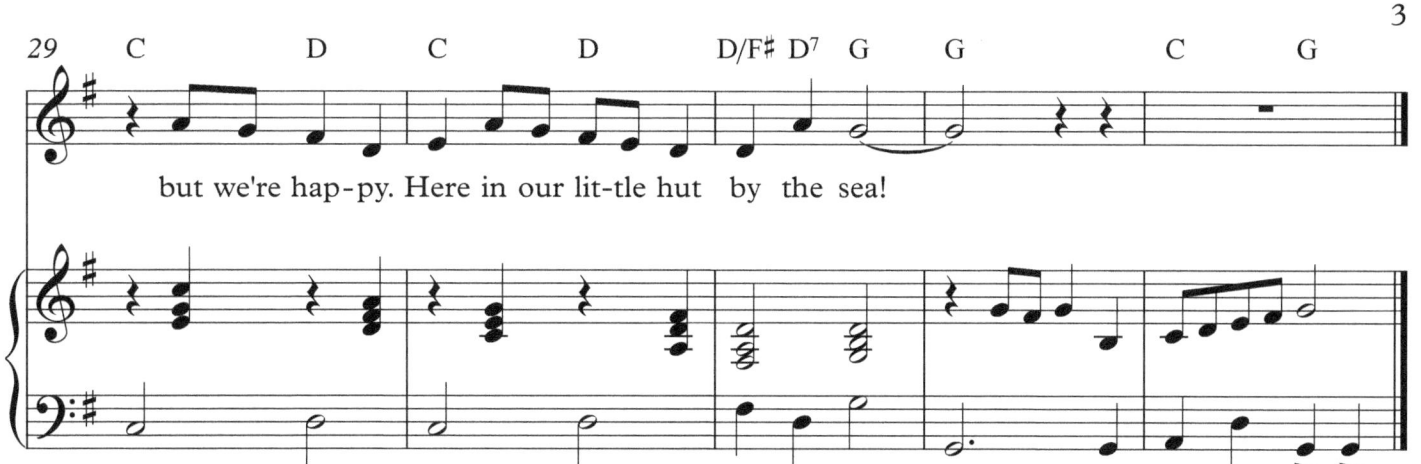

I Couldn't be an Octopus

#3

music and lyrics
Jan Callner

copyright 1984 Jan Callner

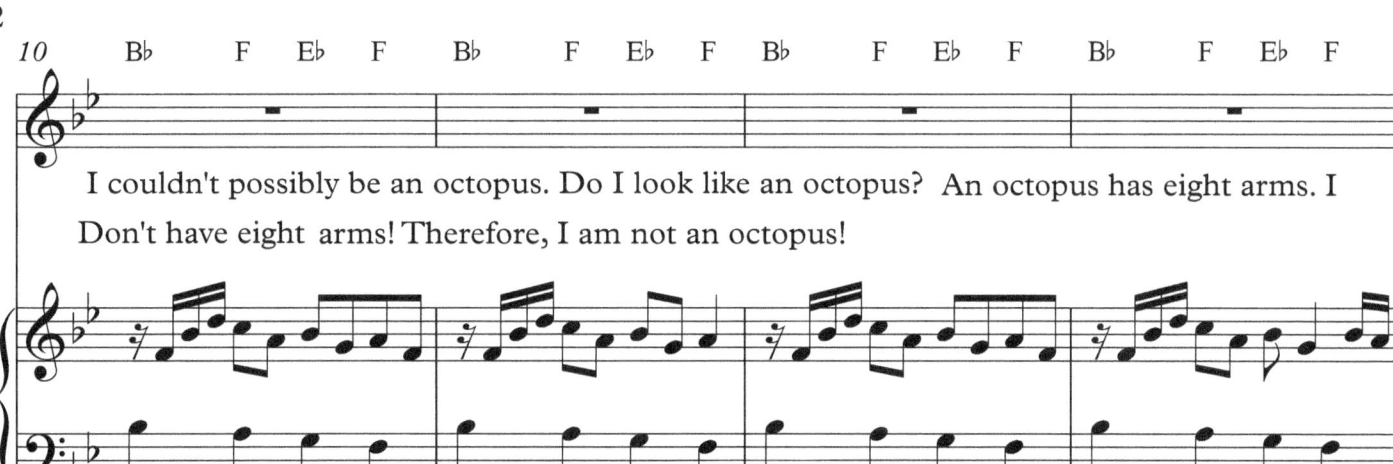
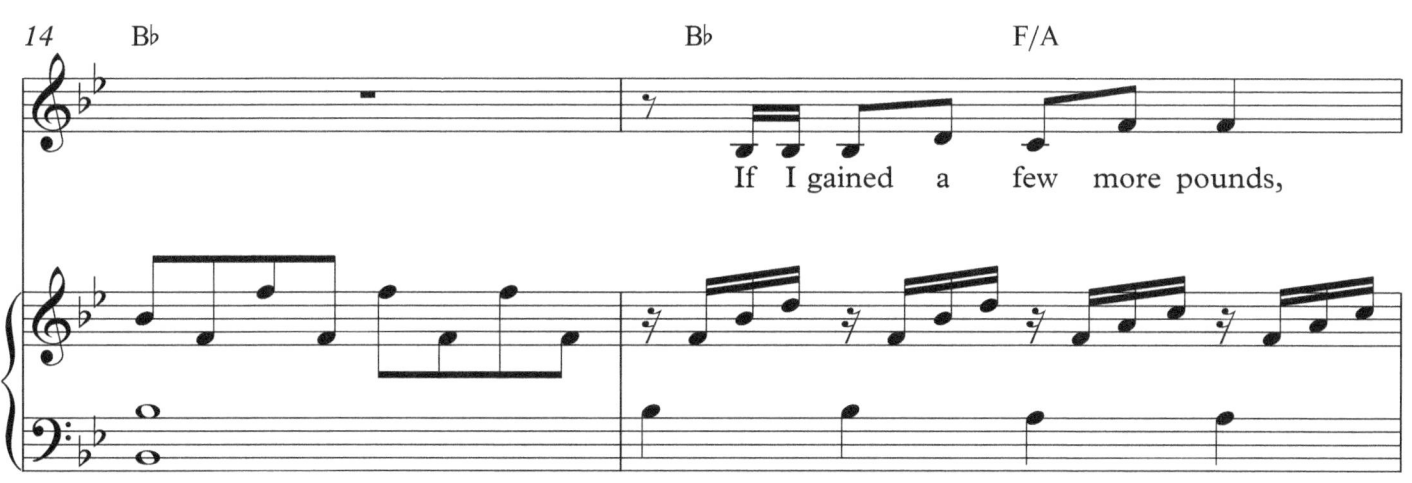
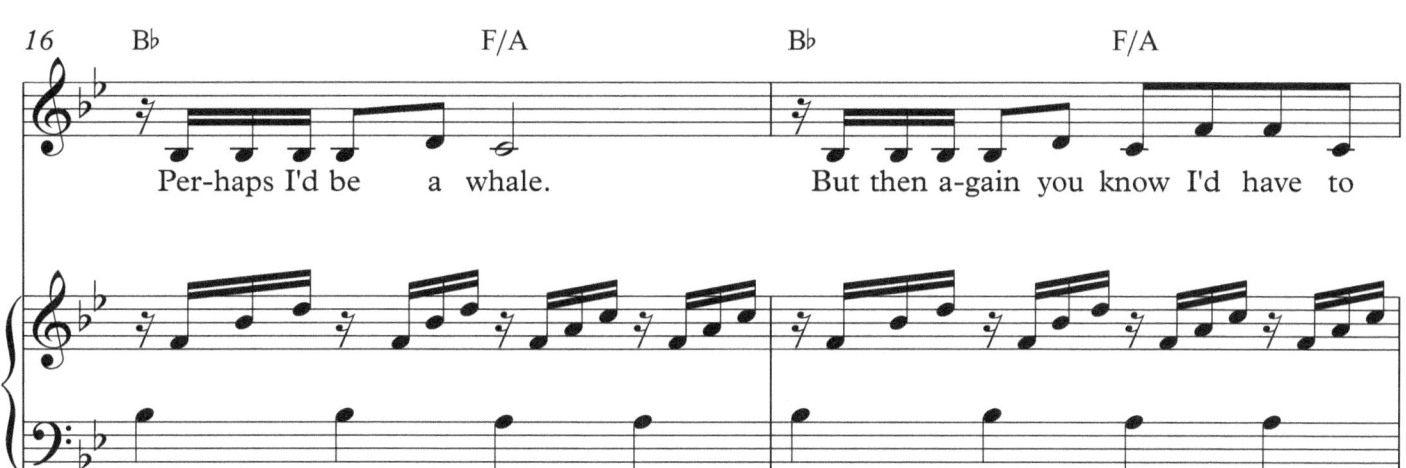

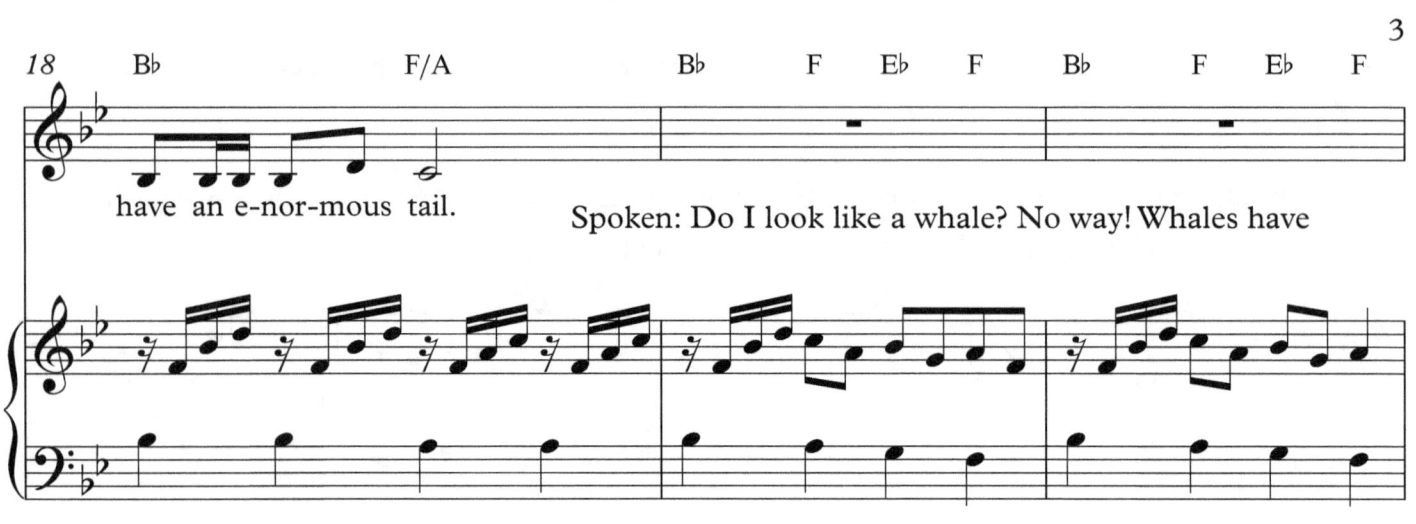

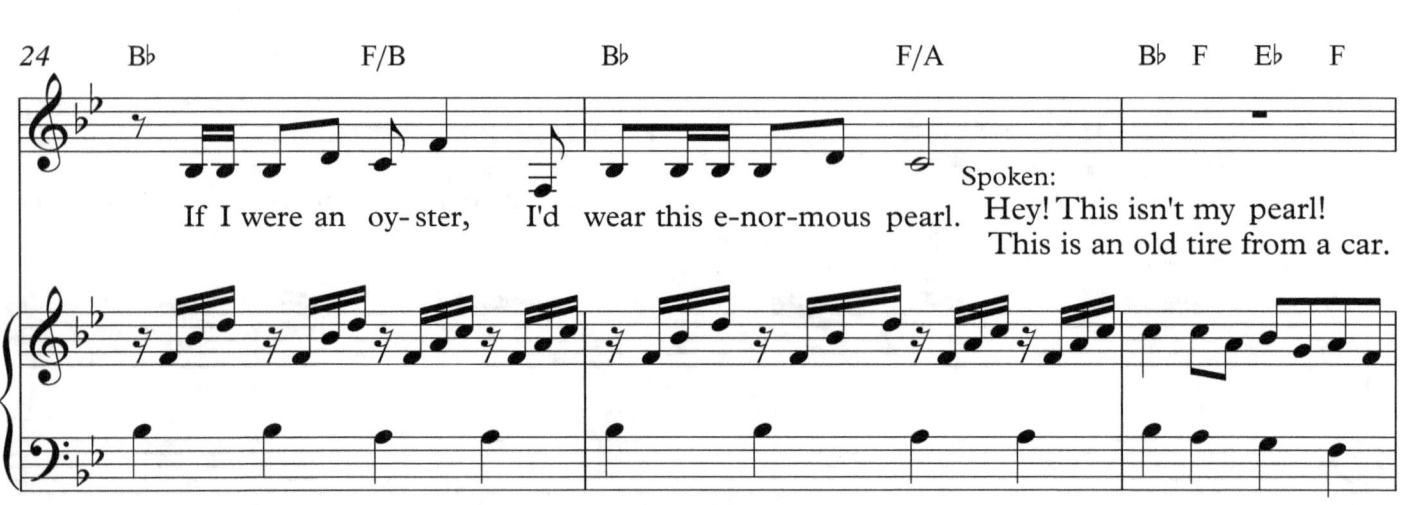

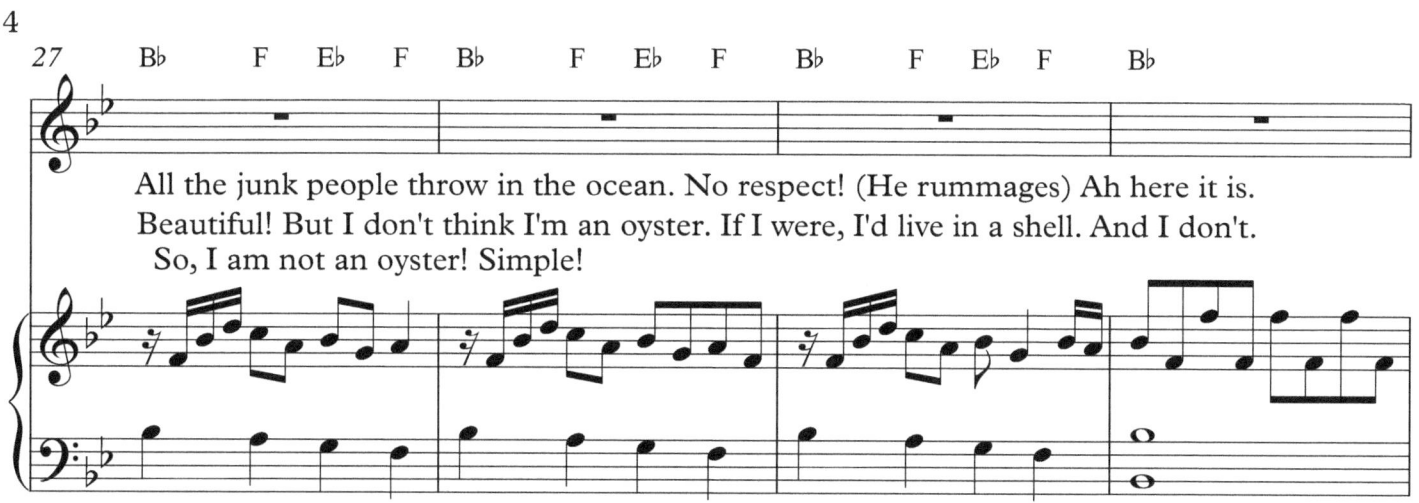

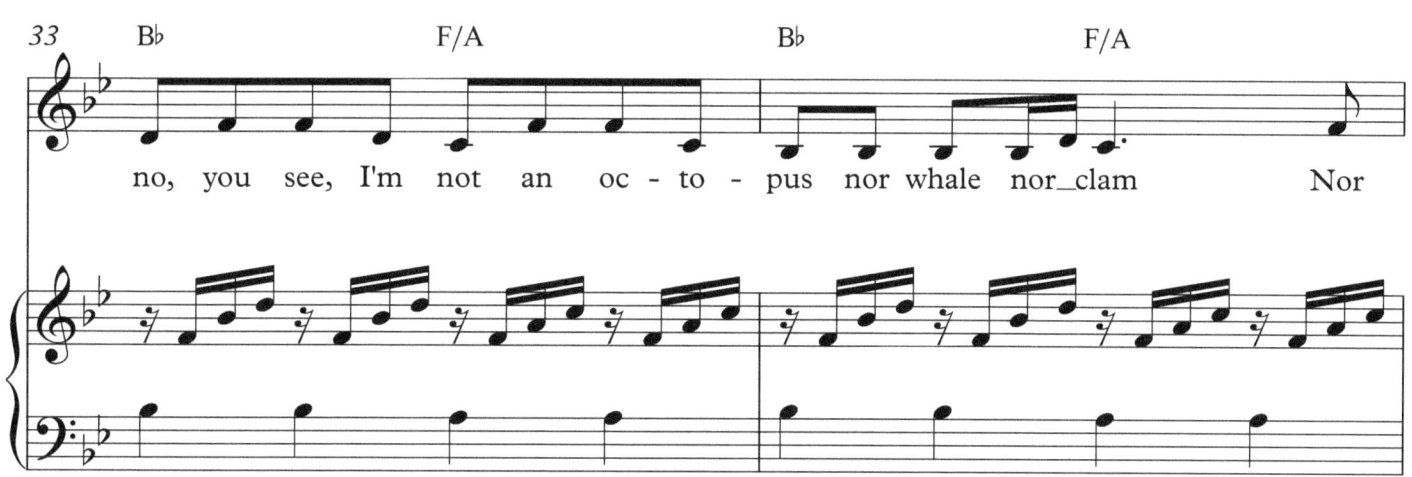

Just One Wish

#4

Words and Music
Jan Callner

copyright 1984 Jan Callner
mike and me productions

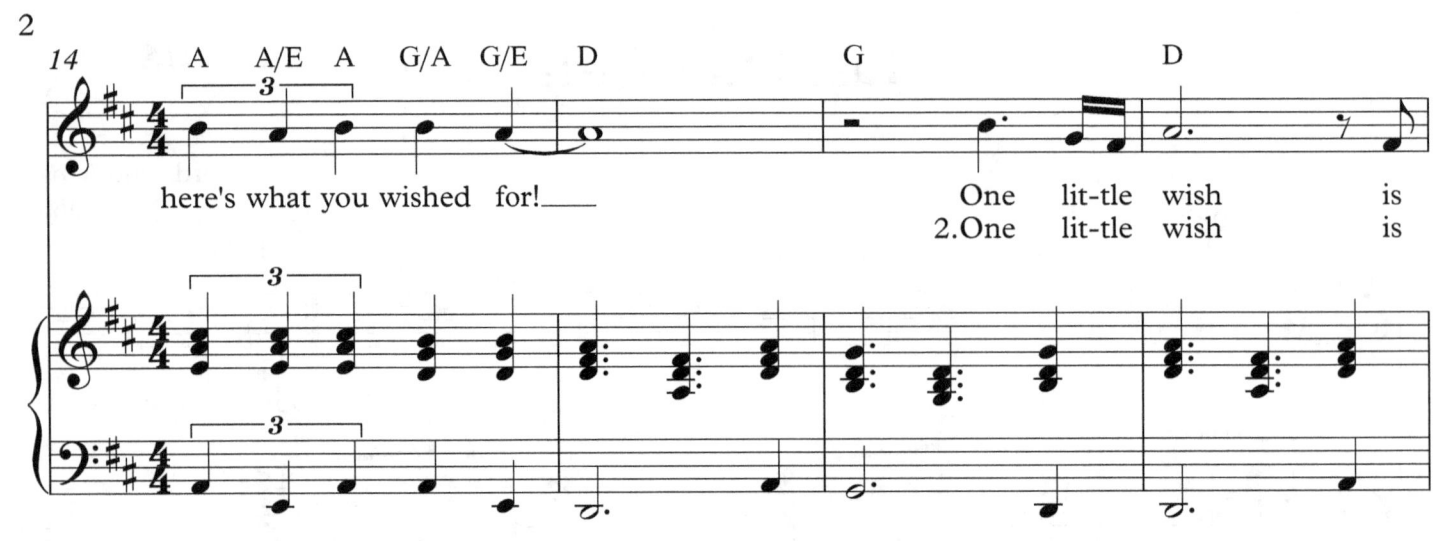
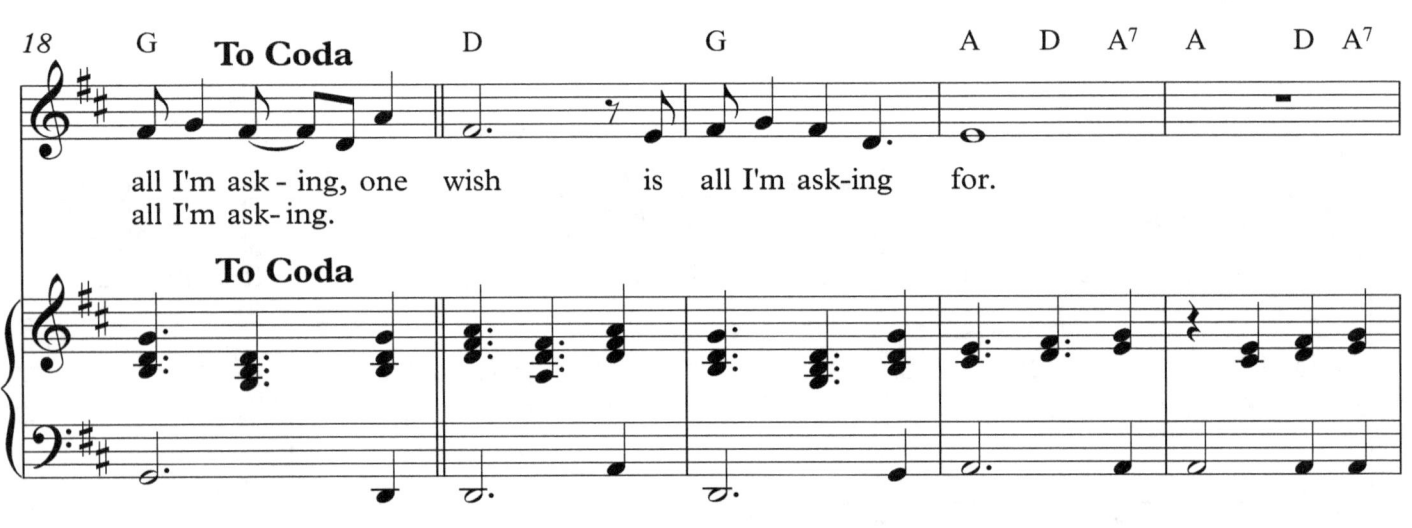

Good Husband

#5

words and music
Jan Callner

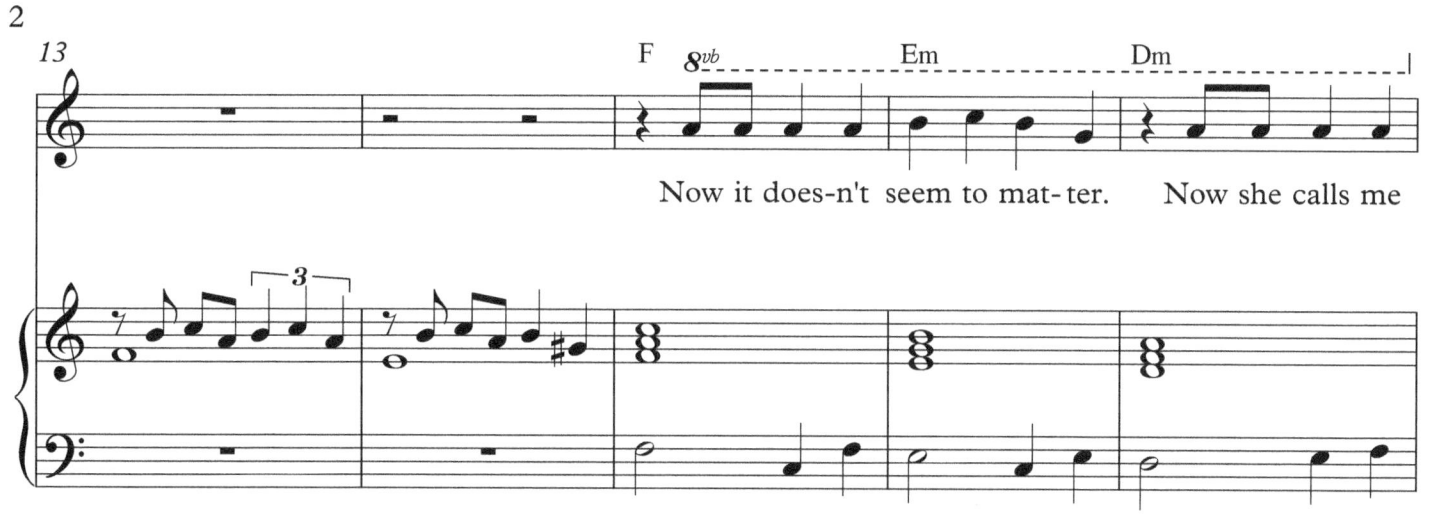
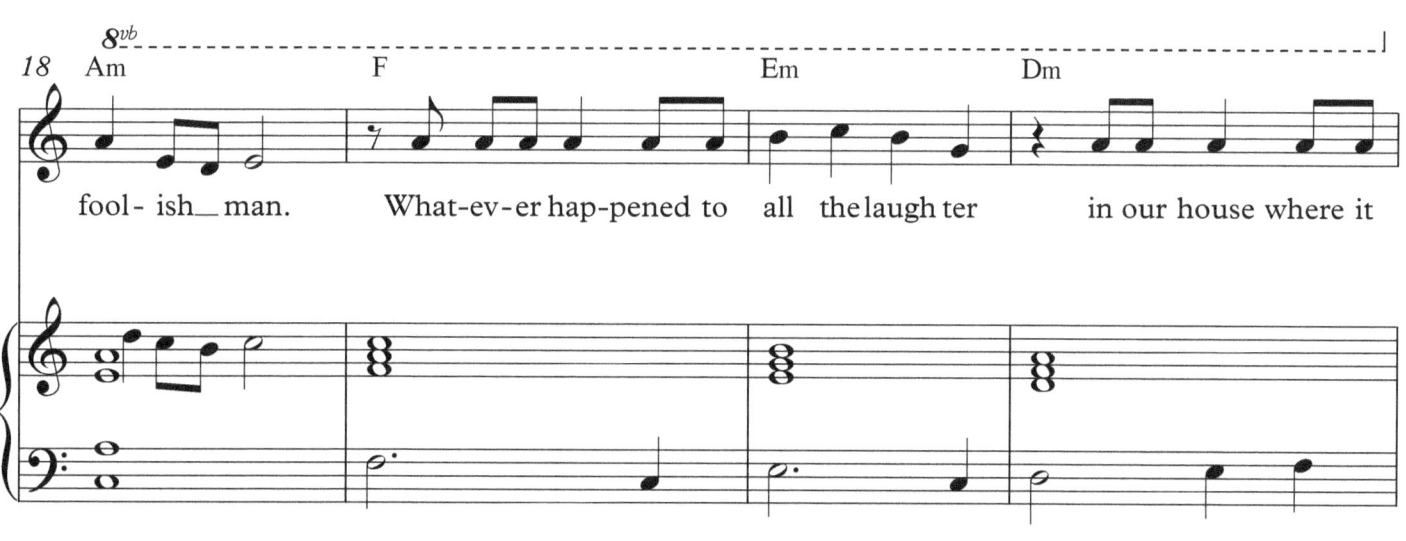
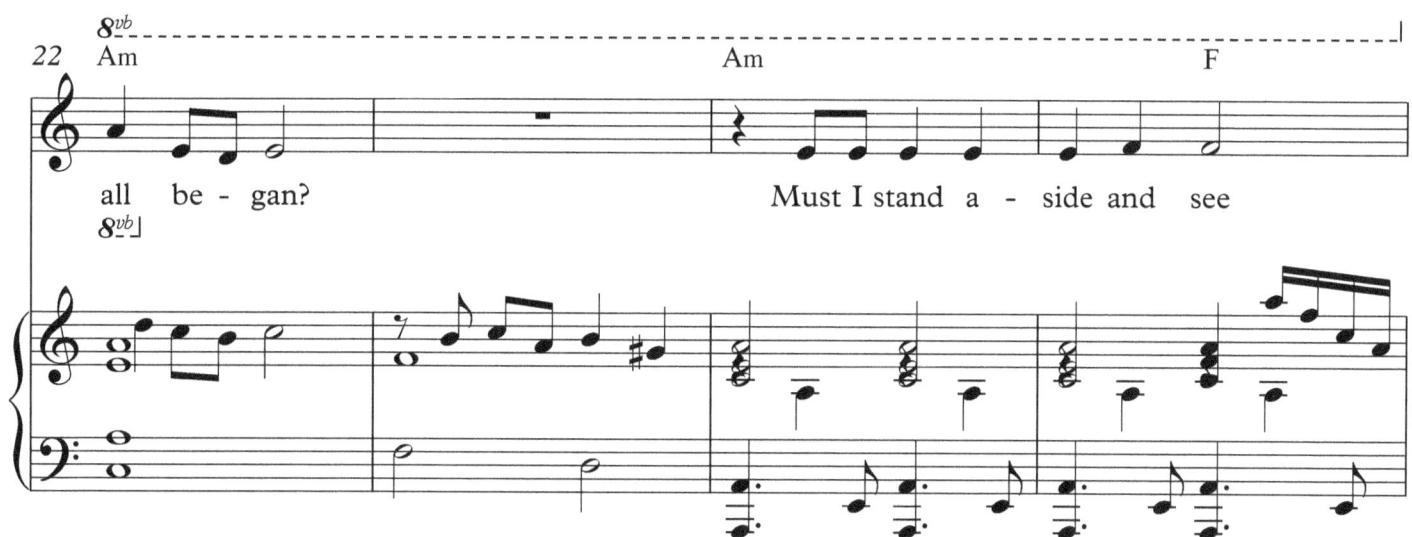

Minor Masterpiece
for Piano

#6

arr. by Jan Callner

J.J. Mouret and Paul Parnes

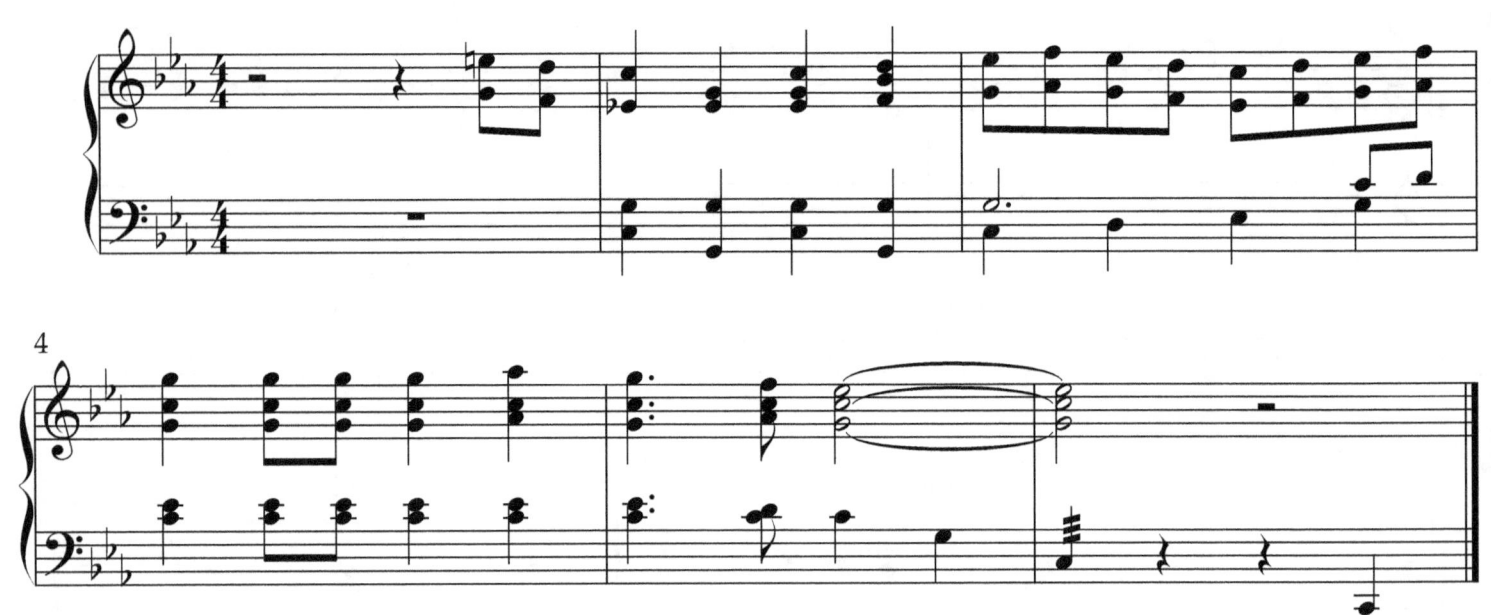

Copyright © 2023 by [Copyright Holder]

Royal Music
incidental

126

#7

Jan Callner

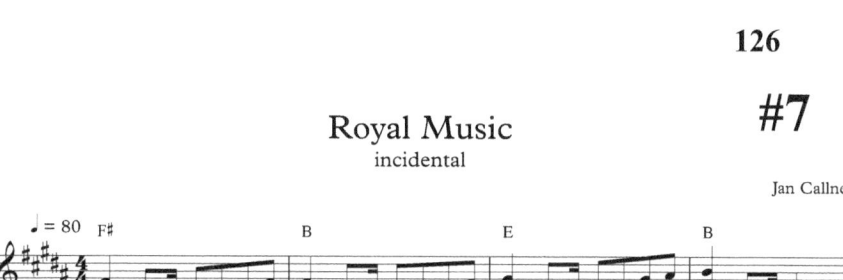

What Do You Do?

#8a

words and music
Jan Callner

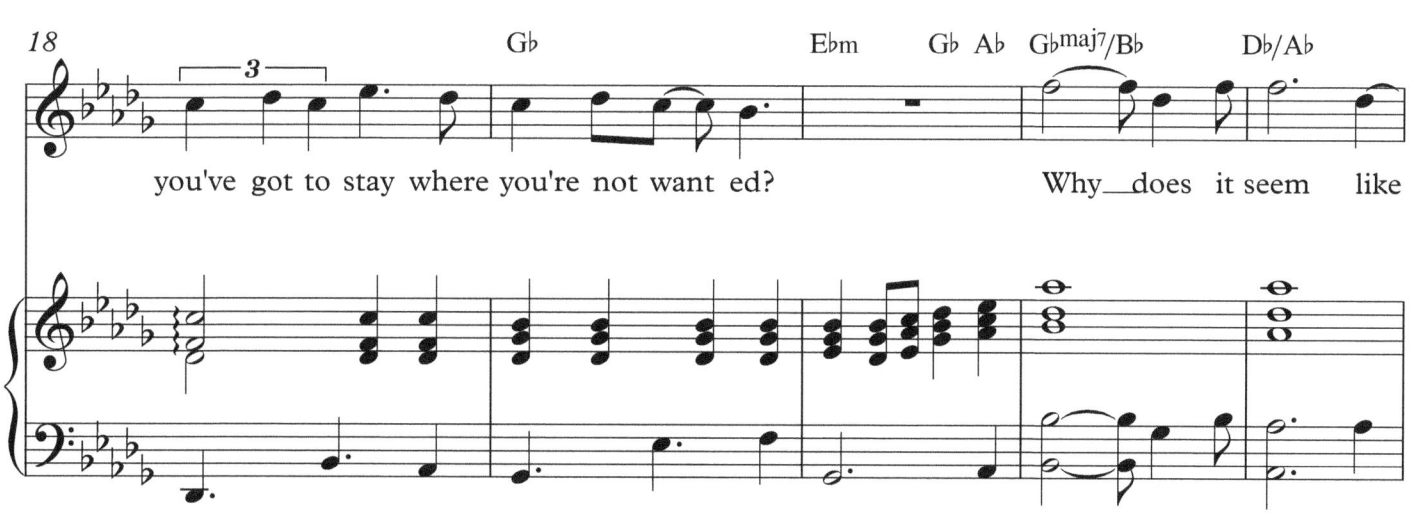

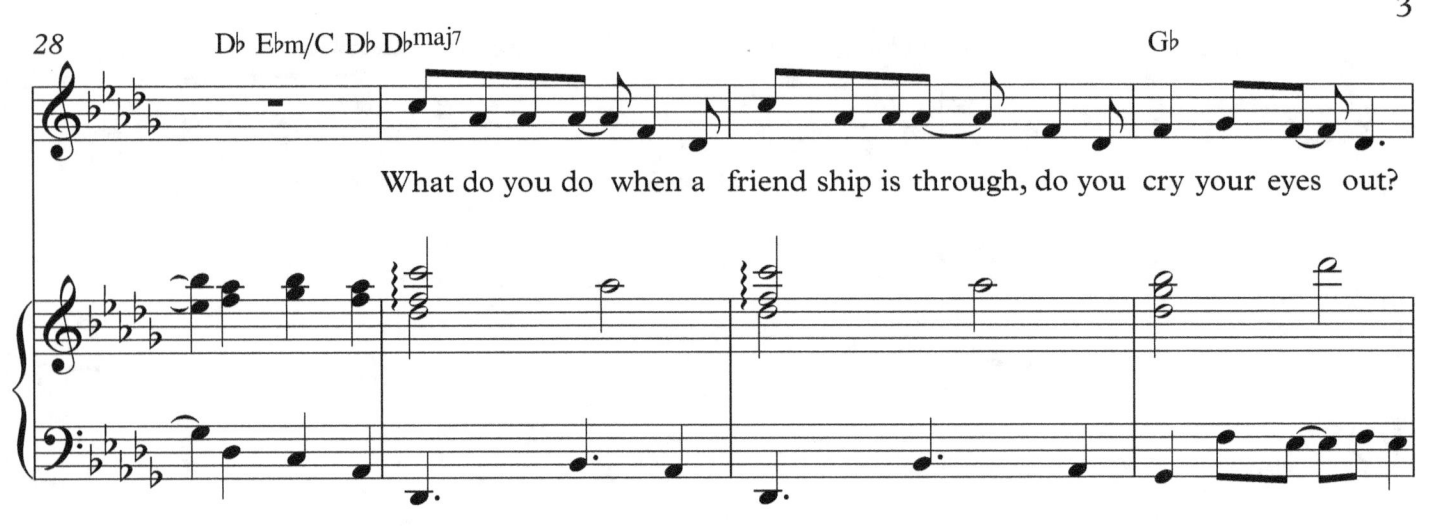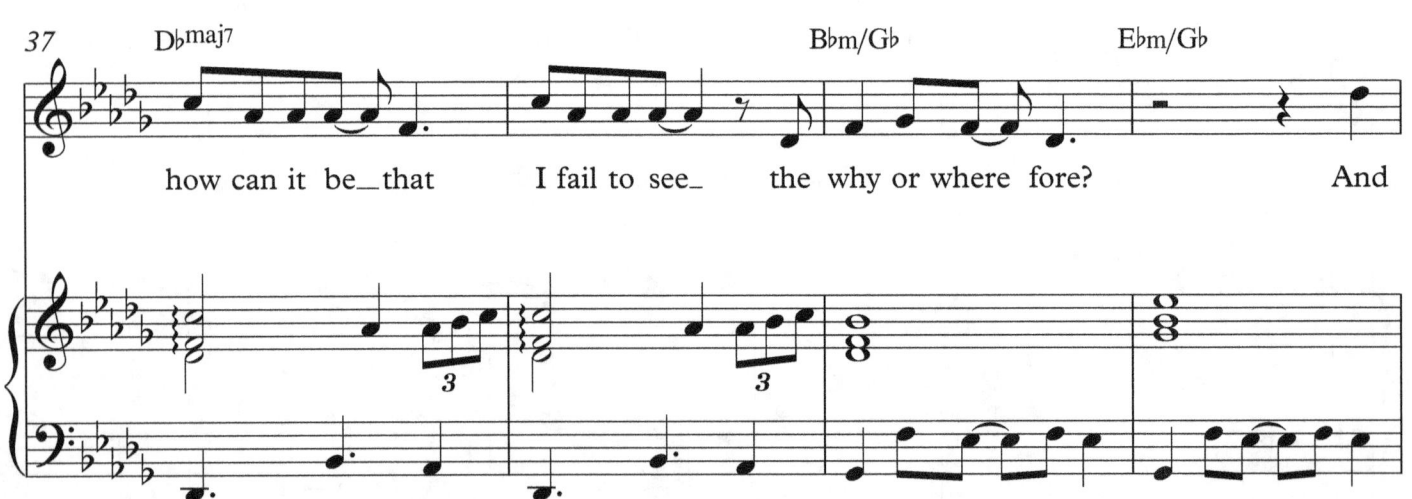

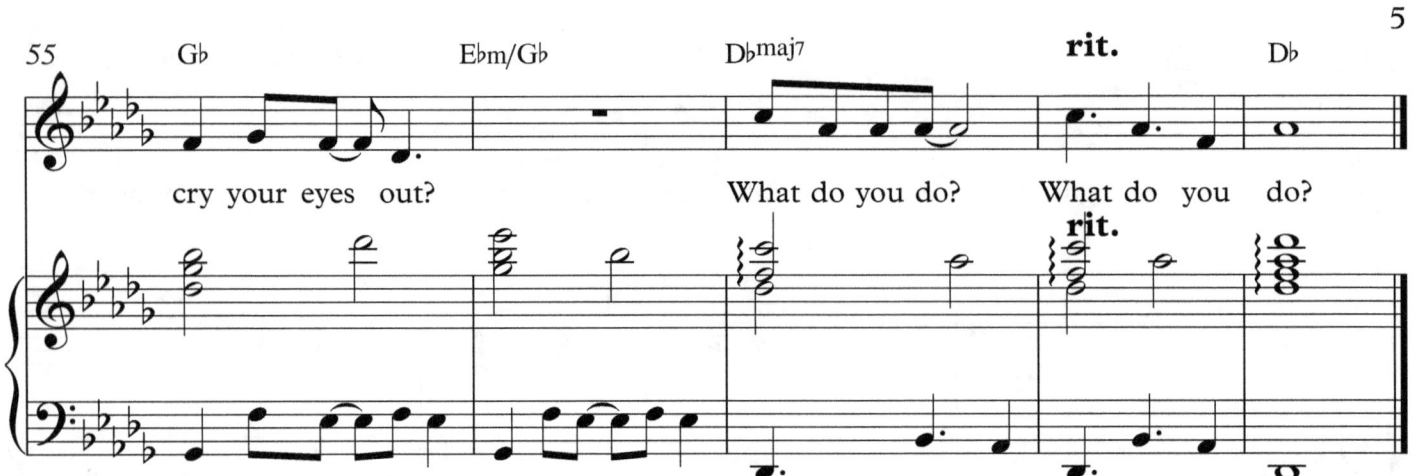

What Do You Do?

#8b

words and music
Jan Callner

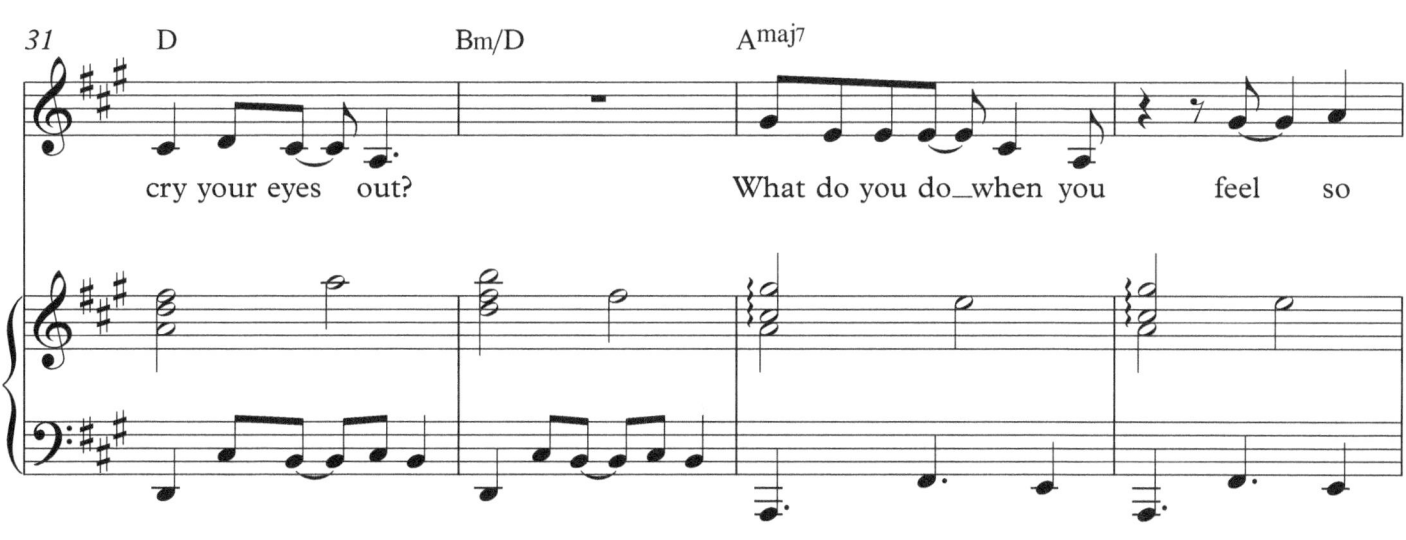

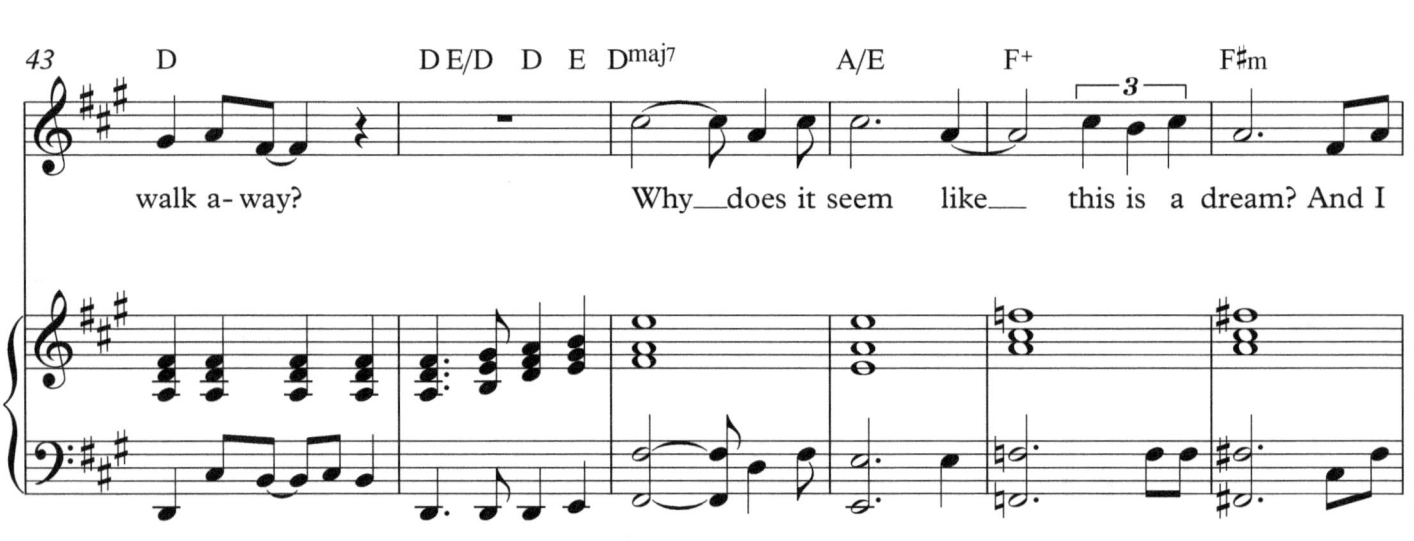

Sun and Moon Dance & Confusion

#9

138

House by the Sea
The Day Was Night

Words and Music
by Jan Callner

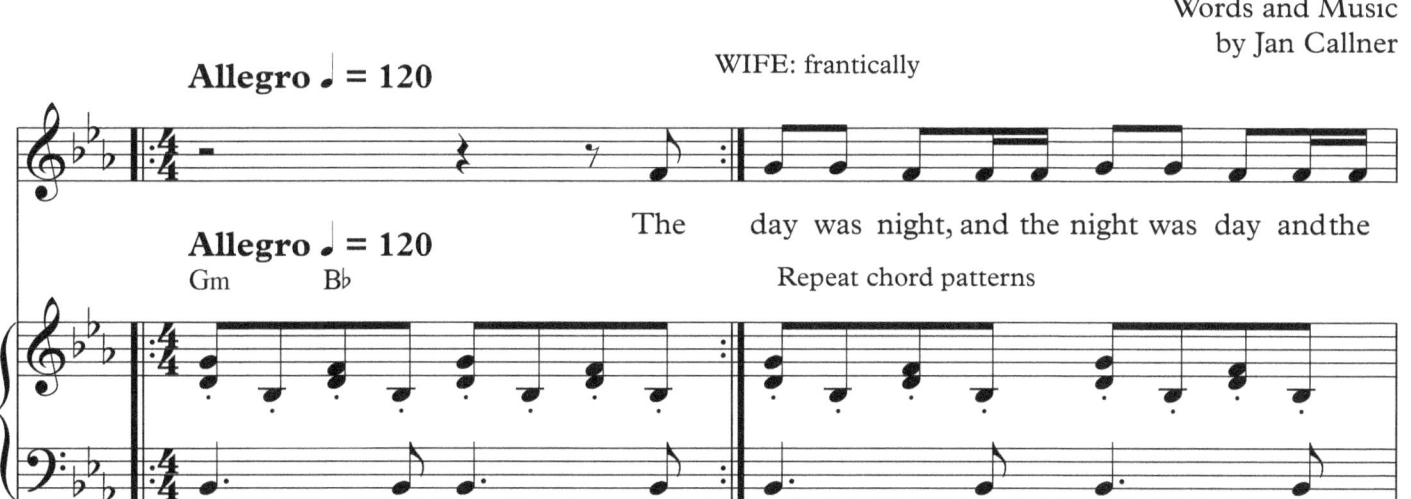
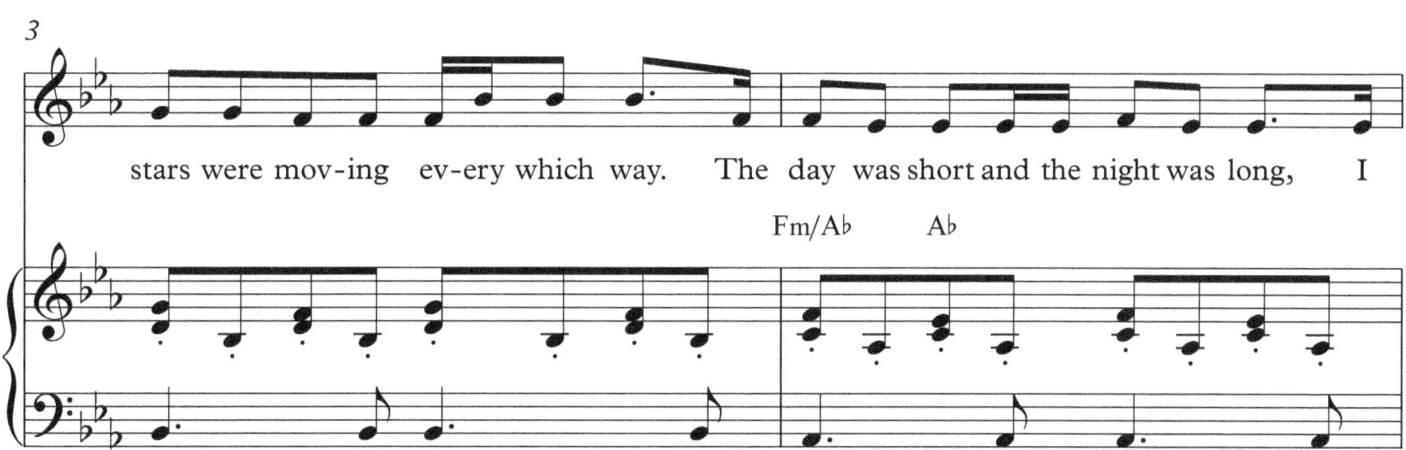
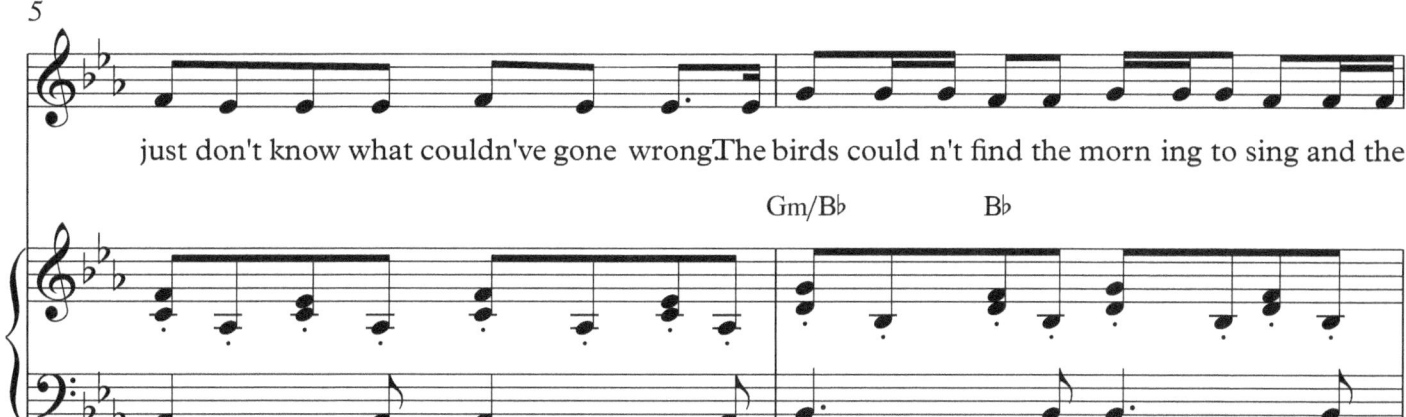

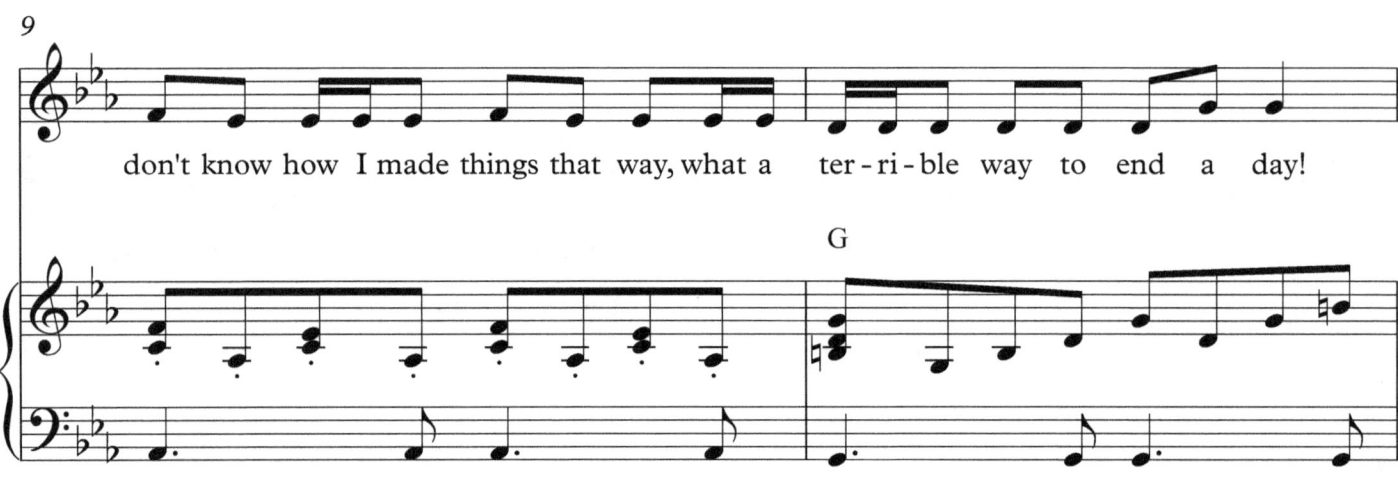
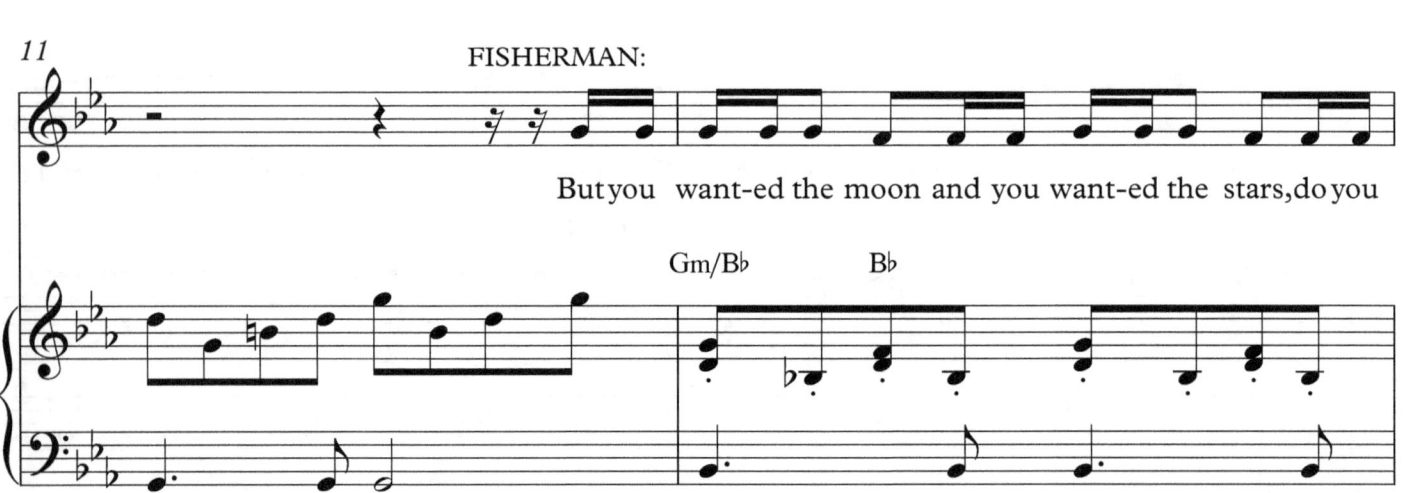

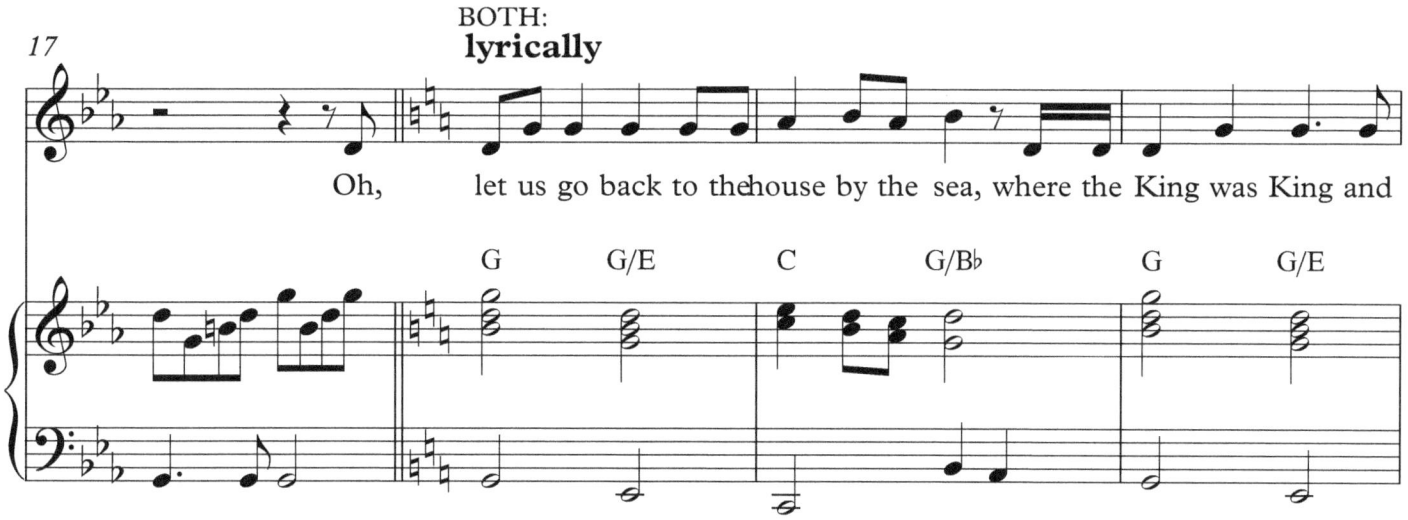

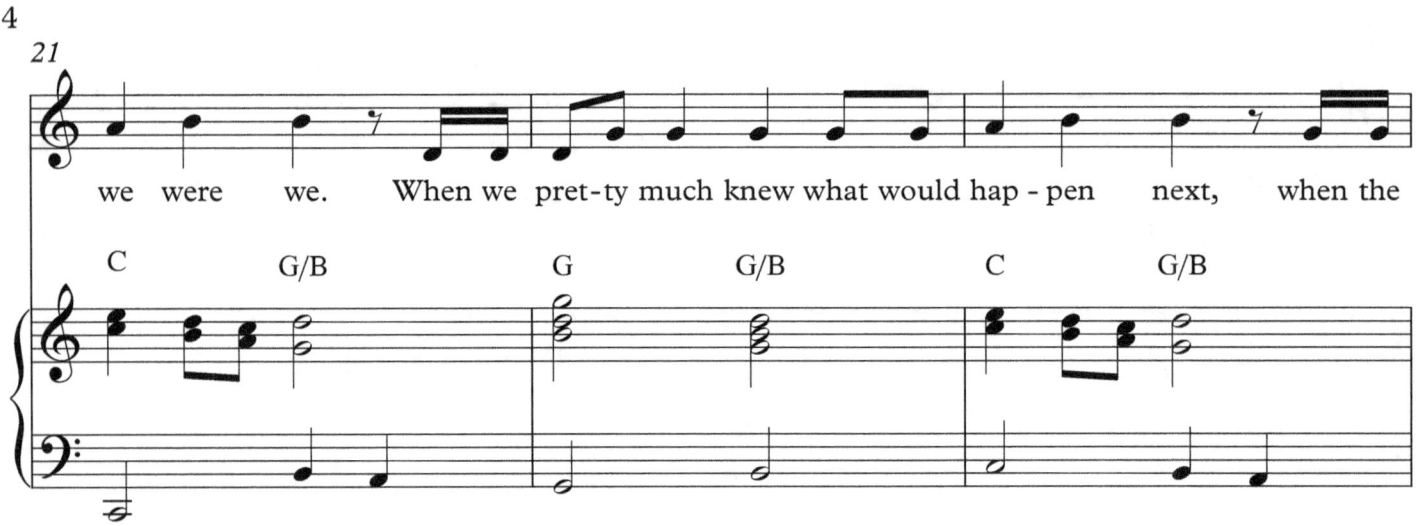
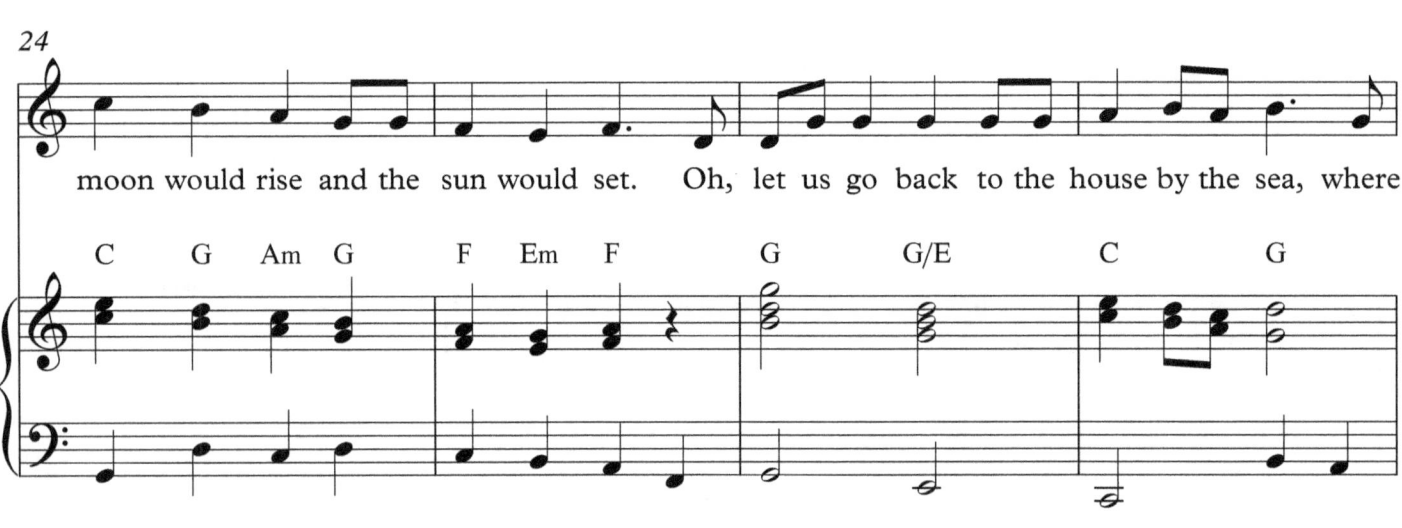

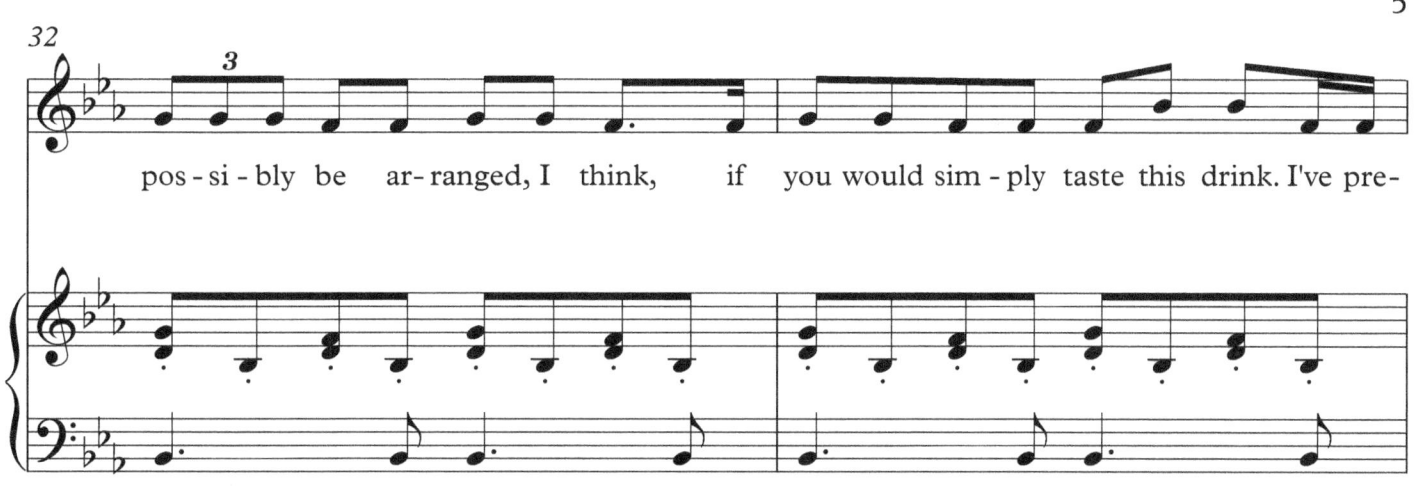
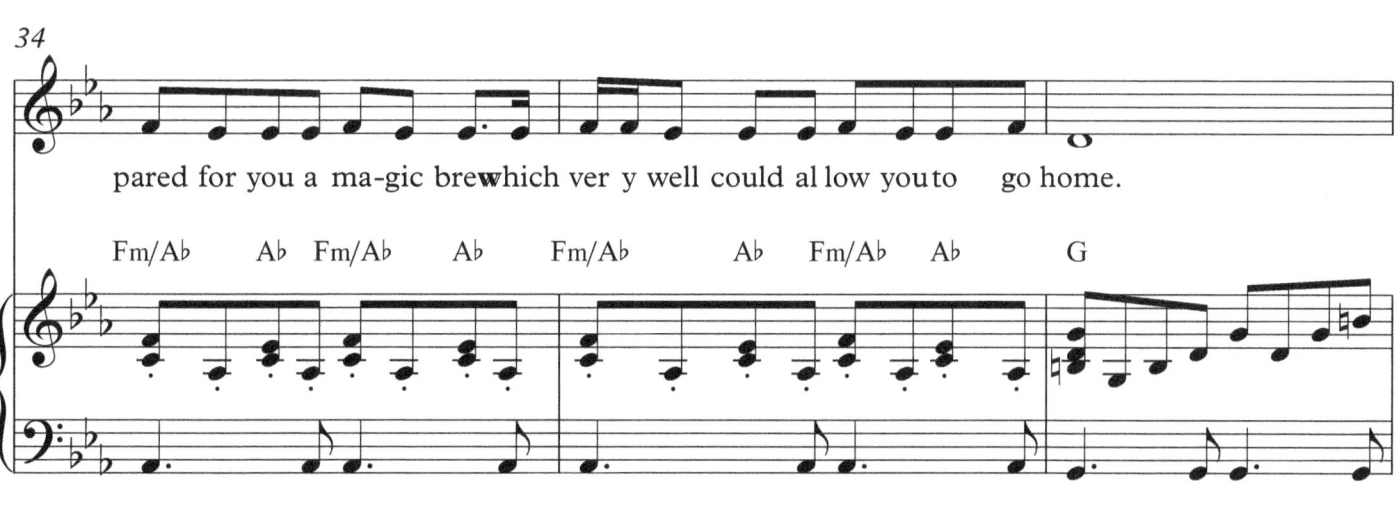
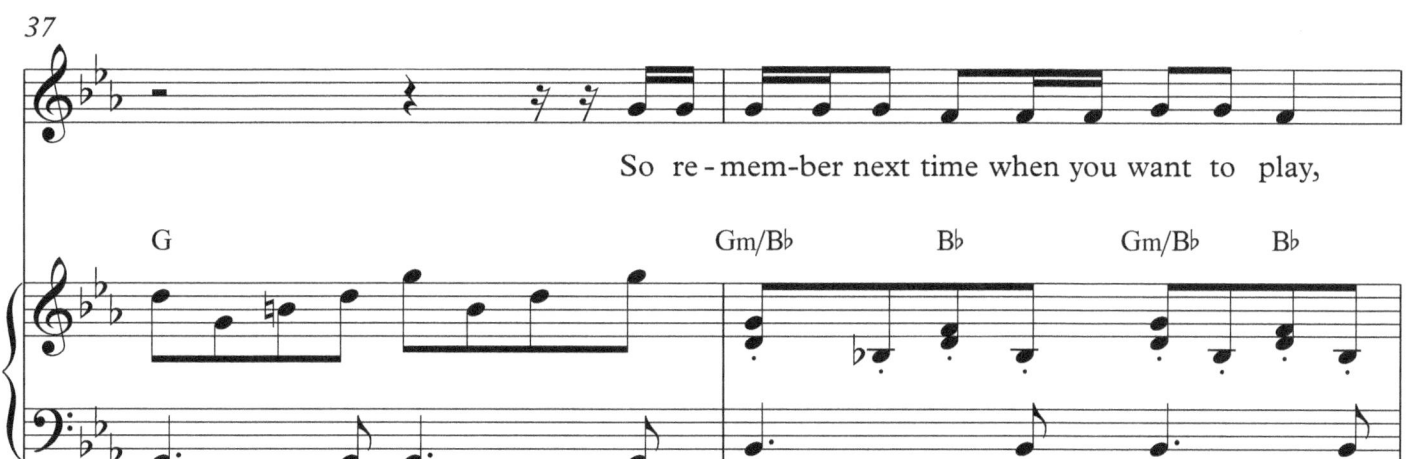

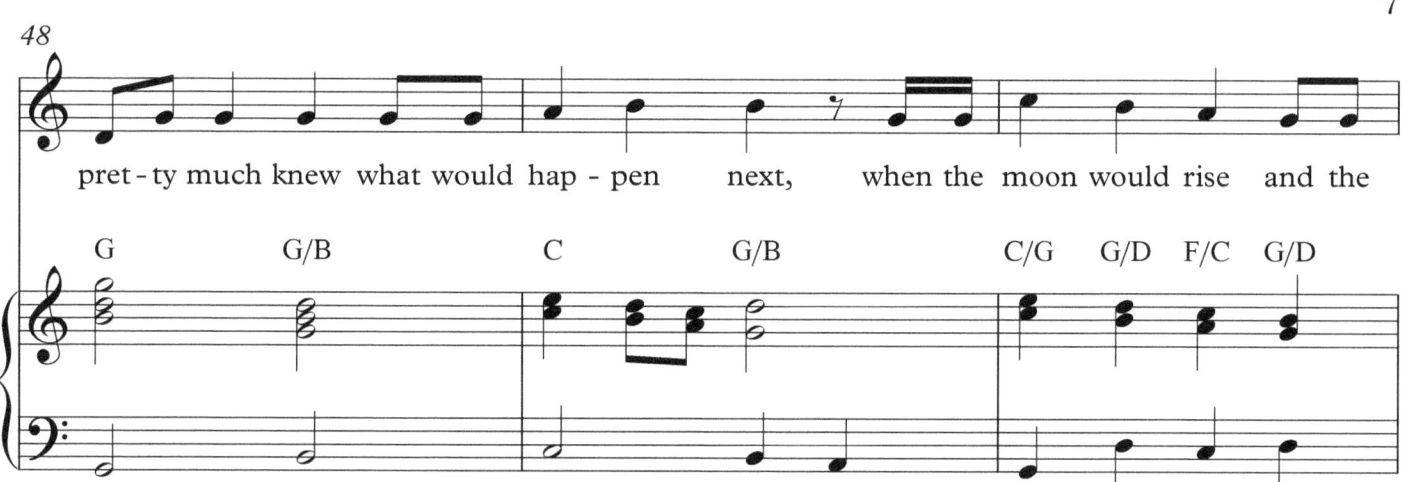

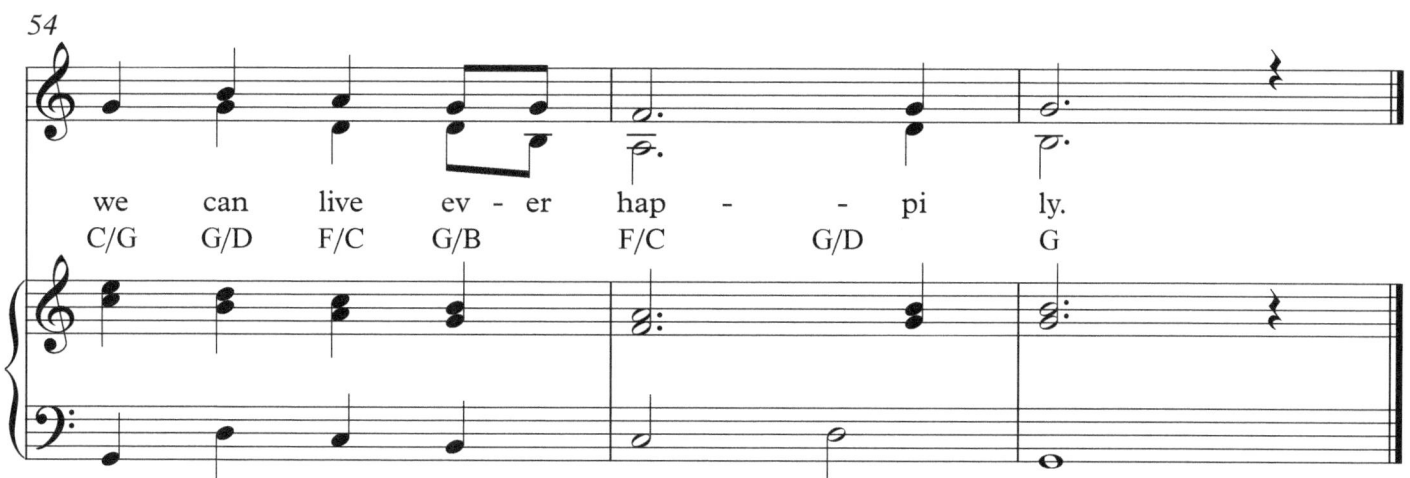

Largo
from The New World Symphony

Antonin Dvorak

Little Hut by the Sea

#12

Words and Music
Jan Callner

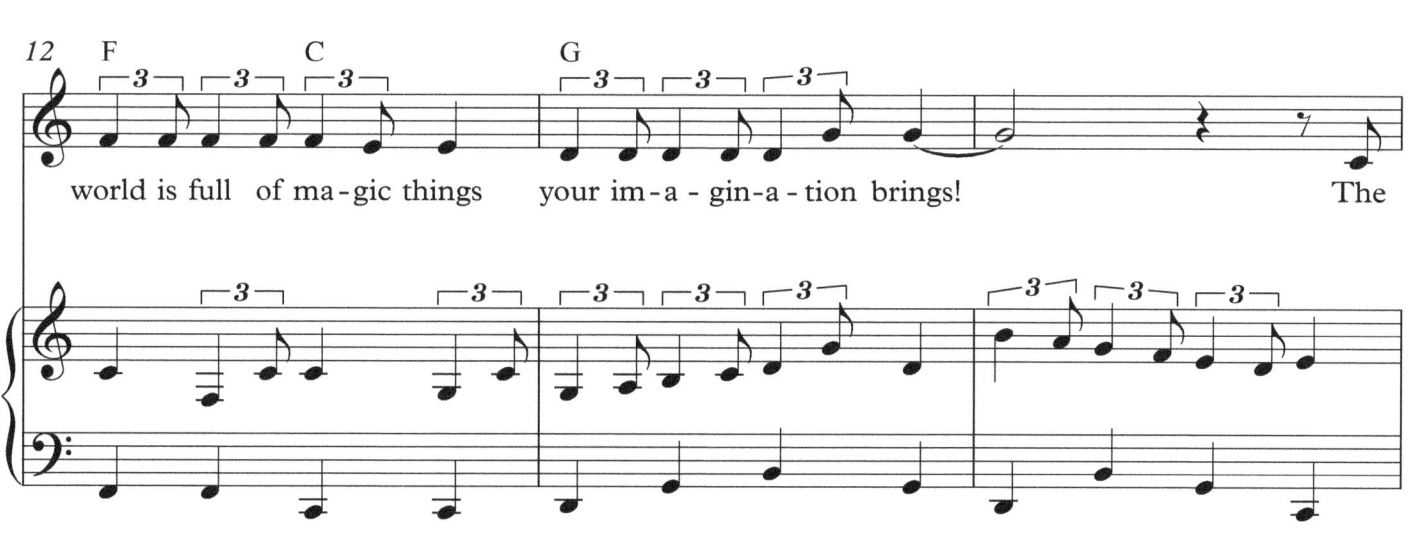
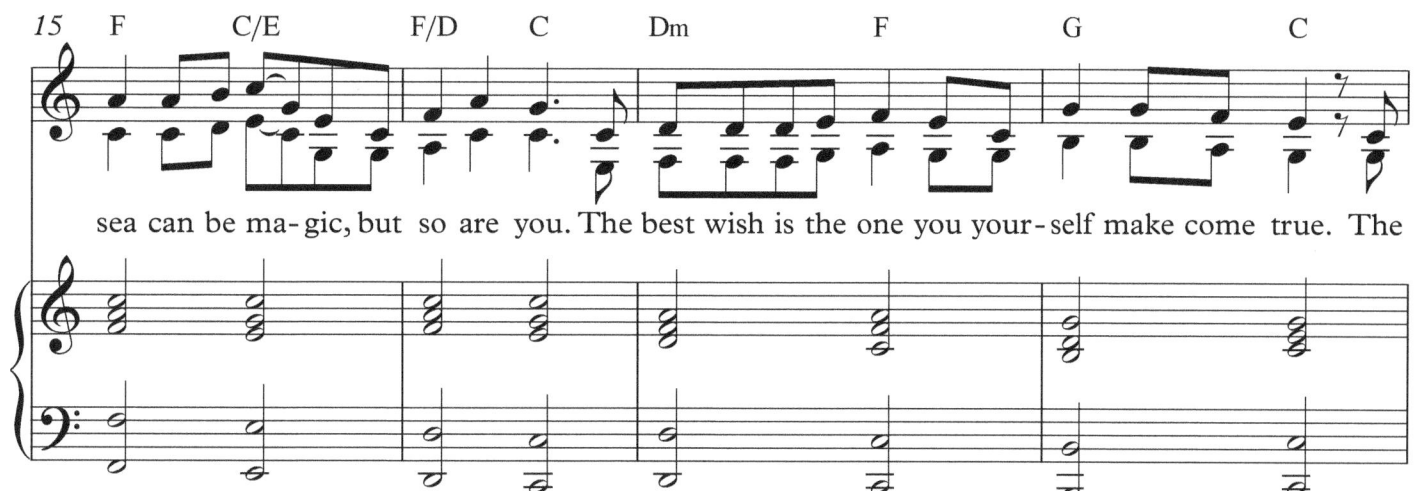

FAN MAIL

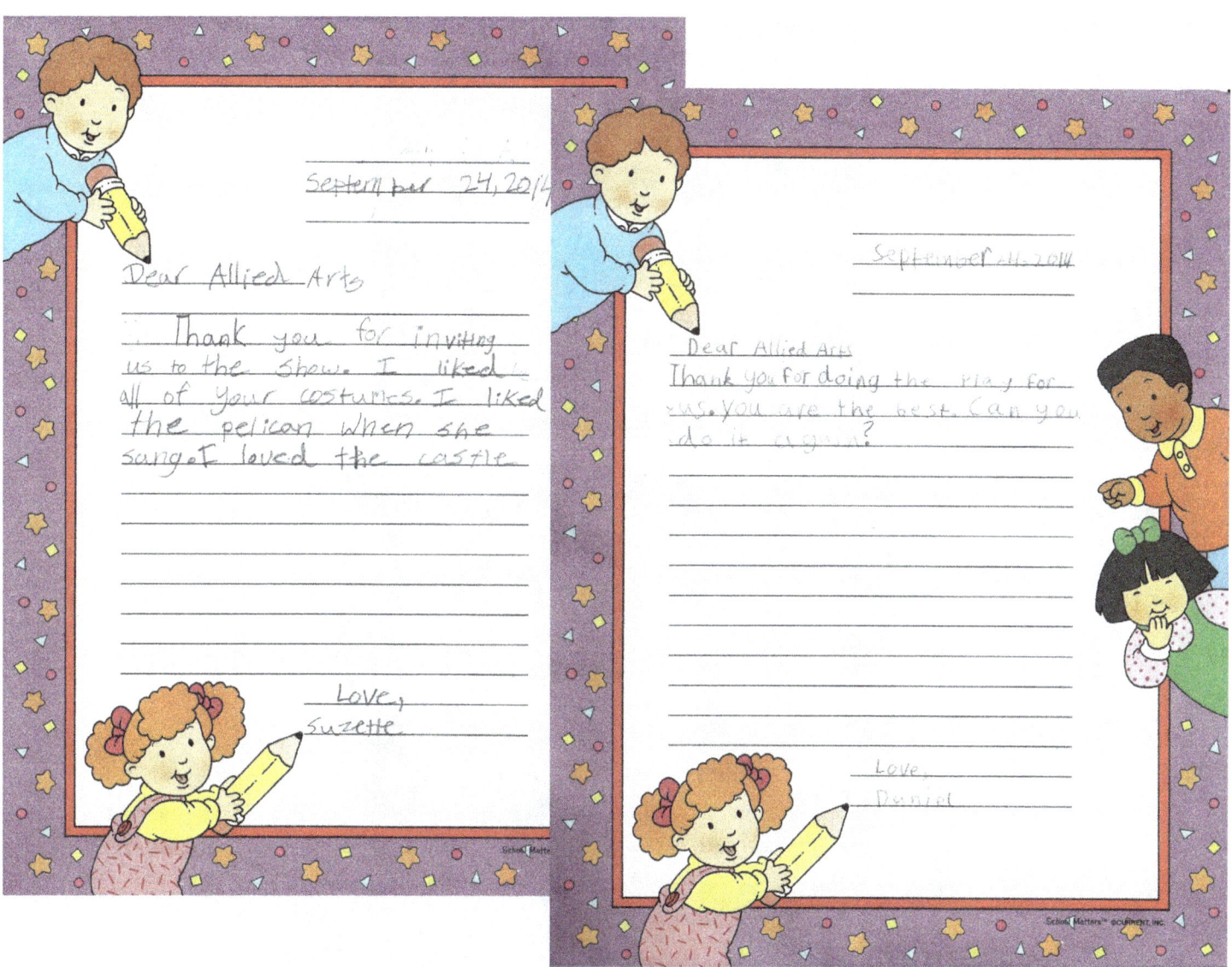

September 24, 2014

Dear Allied Arts,

Thank you for inviting us to the show. I liked all of your costumes. I liked the pelican when she sang. I loved the castle

Love,
Suzette

September 11, 2014

Dear Allied Arts,
Thank you for doing the play for us. You are the best. Can you do it again?

Love,
Daniel

HUT

COTTAGE

MANSION

CASTLE

FEE FIE FOE FUM...JACK'S TALE

Cover Art by Christine Boyka Kluge

Book by Bill Wheeler and Jan Callner

Music and Lyrics by Jan Callner

copyright 2006, 2013 , 2025

FEE FIE FOE FUM...JACK'S TALE

CAST

JACK JACKSON JR.	A SON
JACKLYN JACKSON	A MOTHER
JACK SPRAT	A NEIGHBOR
FANNY SPRAT	A NEIGHBOR
PENELOPE	A COW
JILL	A GIRL IN SEARCH
L.L. BEAN	A BEAN MAN
WITCH	A WITCH
GIANT	A GIANT
YOUNGMAN	A HEN
HARPY	A SINGING HARP

The roles of L.L. and Youngman can be played by the same actor.

The roles of Penelope and Harpy can be played by the same actress.

MUSICAL NUMBERS

#1. YOU STARTED IT — JACK AND FANNY SPRAT

#2. BEST BUDDY — JACK AND PENELOPE

#3. TEA FOR TWO — INSTRUMENTAL

#4. THE BEAN SONG — L.L. BEAN

#5. BEST BUDDY REPRISE — JACK AND PENELOPE

#6. MAGIC — THE WITCH and ALL

#7. JACK COME BACK — THE MOM and ALL

#8. HARPY'S SONG — THE HARP

#9. BEST BUDDY 2ND REPRISE — ALL

#10. FEE, FIE, FOE, FUM — ENTIRE CAST

Scene 1

THERE ARE TWO COTTAGES ON STAGE. ONE IS THE JACKSON HOUSE.

BEANMAN: This is the city, Jacktown. Actually, it's not a city at all. It's a town and this is a tiny neighborhood development named Horner's Corners at the intersection of Nimble Boulevard and Jackla Lane. These are the houses that Jack built. The house on the right is currently unoccupied. It has recently been sold to the Sprats.

The house on the left is the home of the Jackson family; Jacklyn Jackson and her son little Jack Jackson, Jr., a poor but honest family who has been down on its luck since Jack Sr. met with an untimely demise.

JACKLYN ENTERS FROM HER HOUSE

As we join them now, Jacklyn must discuss a family dilemma with her son.

MOM: (Calling offstage) Jack! Jack Darlin'! Stop playing with that cow and come here a moment, will you?

JACK: I'll be right there

COW: Moo, moo! (meaning: Me too!)

MOM: Leave the cow in the field.

COW: Moo! (Rats!)

JACK: (Enters) Mornin' Mom.

MOM: Jack, I have something important to discuss with you.

JACK: You do?

MOM: Yes.

JACK: What is it?

MOM: After breakfast you will have to go into town.

JACK: I will?

MOM: Yes.

JACK:	Why?
MOM:	Now, Jack this is going to be very hard for you, but you must try to understand. We have no more food and we have no more money. Since your poor Father's untimely demise we are very poor. We have already sold all our furniture, and now all that money is gone. We have only one more thing to sell. I love the cow as much as you do, but we have no choice. You must take her to town and sell her!
JACK:	Sell Penelope! Oh, Mother, I can't!
MOM:	But you must, Jack.
JACK:	Penelope is my best friend!
MOM:	I wouldn't make you do this if I didn't have to. I know it hurts something terrible. Now, I want you to brush her and make her look as fine as possible.
JACK:	But what are we going to do for milk?
MOM:	Milk isn't only thing we need Jack, and, besides, if you get a good enough price for her, we'll be able to afford to buy milk.
JACK:	All right, Mom. I'll do it.
MOM:	Thank you, Jack. I love you very much.
JACK:	I love you too, Mom
PENELOPE:	(from offstage) Moo, Moo, Moo! (Oh Jack! Jack!)
MOM:	Now go and get Penelope ready. (Jack exits.) You're a good son, Jack Jackson, Jr..

MOM EXITS INTO HOUSE. THE SPRATS ENTER CARRYING THEIR LUGGAGE.

J.S.:	Well, here we are! Our new home!
FANNY:	A Jackbuilt house! It has always been my dream to live in a house that Jack built! I just hope our neighbors here are better than our last neighbors.
J.S.:	Oh, don't start that again.
FANNY:	I'm sorry, but Mrs. Peter was a very nice woman and I don't think she deserved to be locked up in that pumpkin shell!

J.S.:	Look, Peter Peter is one of my best friends, and we don't know everything that went on between them. Besides, he may have put her in that pumpkin shell, but he kept her there very well! So don't criticize my friends!
FANNY:	Ha! Some friends. Peter Peter! And that little thief Tom Tom.
J.S.:	Can't you just forgive and forget? He was just a kid when he stole that pig and ran away. What about your friends? There are some real prizes there! Mary Contrary going on and on about her garden! And that ridiculous Lillybelle Muffet! Honestly, a grown woman who faints at the sight of a spider!
FANNY:	Leave my friends out of this!
J.S.:	Well, you started it!
	MUSIC STARTS
FANNY:	I did not!
J.S.:	You most certainly did!

SONG #1: YOU STARTED IT

FANNY:	**(Singing) You started it!**
J.S.:	**(Singing) Did not.**
FANNY:	**You always start it!**
J.S.:	**Do not!**
FANNY:	**I'm always right.**
J.S.:	**You're not.**
FANNY:	**You're always wrong!**
J.S.:	**Am not! The sky is blue.**
FANNY:	**The sky is gray.**
J.S.:	**You always get your own way.**
FANNY:	**Do not!**
J.S.:	**Do so!**
FANNY:	**Do not!**

J.S.:	Do so!
FANNY:	Do not, not, not, not, not!
J.S.:	Do so, so, so, so, so!
FANNY:	Do not, not, not, not, not.
J.S.:	Do so, so, so, so, so!
FANNY:	I'm more observant.
J.S.:	You're blind!
FANNY:	You're callous!
J.S.:	I'm kind.
FANNY:	The sea is green.
J.S.:	The sea is blue.
FANNY:	Life would be sweeter without you!
J.S.:	I doubt that.
FANNY:	It's true!
J.S.:	You must be joking.
FANNY:	The joke's on you.
J.S.:	You're so charmless
FANNY:	Am not!
J.S.:	Argumentative!
FANNY:	What rot!
J.S.:	So very lovely!
FANNY:	Am not!
J.S.:	Gotcha! You started it!
FANNY:	Did not!
J.S.:	You always start it!

FANNY:	Do not! Do not, not!
J.S.:	Do so!
FANNY:	Do not, not!
J.S.:	Do so!
FANNY:	Do not!
J.S.:	Do so!
FANNY:	Do not!
J.S.:	Do so!
FANNY:	(Speaking) All right! All right! Let's not argue out here! The neighbors might hear, and we do want to make a good impression.
J.S.:	Okay, okay! Look, someone's coming. Now act presentable, and no arguing!
FANNY:	Well, you started it!
J.S.:	Shhh! (Mom enters)
MOM:	Oh hello! Have you seen a little boy around here anywhere? I've sent my boy Jack on an errand, and I want to make sure he's on his way.
J.S.:	Why no, we haven't seen him. But let us introduce ourselves. I believe we're your new neighbors. I'm Jack Sprat. This is my wife, the lovely…
FANNY:	Fanny Sprat! How do you do?
MOM:	How-dy-doo.
J.S.:	We're just moving in. Looks like a real nice neighborhood.
FANNY:	I bet we'll be happy here.
MOM:	I hope so. And, yes, it is nice and peaceful. As soon as you're all settled in, you'll have to come over for dinner. We don't have much, but we're not as bad off as the Old Hubbard woman down the street. Poor thing…her cupboard's always bare!
J.S.:	We'd be pleased to have dinner with you.
MOM:	And my little boy. There's me, I'm Jacklyn Jackson and my little boy, Jack Jackon, Jr.. My husband, Jack Sr., met an untimely demise a few years ago.

FANNY:	I'm so sorry. What happened?
J.S.:	Fanny!
MOM:	That's all right. It was a freak accident. He was walking past this tall stone wall over on King's Row when, all of a sudden, this gigantic egg fell off the wall just as Jack Sr. was passing by, and…and…and…
FANNY:	He was crushed?
MOM:	Scrambled!
FANNY:	How awful!
MOM:	Yes.
J.S.:	Well, Mrs. Jackson…
MOM:	Jacklyn, please.
J.S.:	Okay, Jacklyn please. Fanny and I would love to have dinner with you and your son. The only thing is, we're on special diets. I can eat no fat, and Fanny here must never have lean. It affects her terribly. Lean makes the lady mean!
FANNY:	Oh Jack!
J.S.:	Well, it does!
MOM:	No problem. We'll just have fruit salad. That way you can lick the platter clean! Well, good luck and welcome to Horner's Corners. I must get back to my housework. If you see my son Jack, please send him on his way to town. (she exits)
J.S.:	Will do. Nice woman.
FANNY:	Very nice.
JACK:	(Enters, calling) Penelope! Here girl! Penny, where are you? C'mon, Penelope, please!
J.S.:	Looking for your dog, Sonny?
JACK:	No, my cow.
FANNY:	Cow?
JACK:	Yes, she's my pet. My best friend. My cow!

FANNY: A pet cow friend.

J.S.: Why not? You must be Jack Jackson, Jr.!

JACK: How did you know?

FANNY: We just met your mother. We're your new neighbors, Jack and Fanny Sprat.

J.S. Your mom told us if we saw you to send you on your way.

JACK: Yes, sir, I know, but I'm just sad…you see, we are very poor.

FANNY: I know, your poor father.

J.S. Fanny!

JACK: That's O.K. Anyway, we are very poor and my Mom is making me sell my cow so we'll have money for food and stuff.

J.S.: But that cow is your pet!

FANNY: Jack…

J.S.: And your friend. It isn't right!

FANNY: It's none of our business!

J.S.: But a boy needs his pet cow friend. Especially when he doesn't have a fa…

FANNY: Jack!

JACK: That's all right Mr. Sprat. My mom is right. It's difficult, but a Jack's gotta do what a Jack's gotta do!

J.S.: (Dabbing his eyes with a handkerchief.) Brave boy!

FANNY: C'mon, Jack. Let's get this stuff inside. (She exits.)

J.S.: You're a good son, Jack Jackson Jr.! (He exits.)

JACK: Penny!

PENNY: (Penny enters) Moo? (What's up?)

JACK: You're my best friend, aren't you?

PENNY: Moo! (Of course I am. Don't be a jerk!)

JACK: And you know I love you, don't you?

PENNY:	Moo…(Oh, oh. Something's wrong.)
JACK:	My mom and I are very poor. We have no food, and all of our money is gone.
PENNY:	(Sniffling a little. Jack dabs her eyes with his handkerchief.) Moo. (That is so sad.)
JACK:	An although I love you very much, I have no choice but to sell you.
PENNY:	WHAT?
JACK:	What?
PENNY:	What!
JACK:	What! You spoke!
PENNY:	SO!
JACK:	So! You've never spoken before!
PENNY:	You never said you were going to sell me before! What do you mean SELL ME?
JACK:	Aw, Penny, try and understand. If there were any other way I wouldn't do this. But I have to.
PENNY:	But, Jack, I love you. I don't want to leave. You're my best friend
JACK:	I love you too and I don't want you to leave. You know, just because we won't be together doesn't mean we won't be friends.
JACK:	**SONG #2: BEST BUDDY** **Looks like we have to part ways.** **Sure wish that you could have stayed.** **You'll take the high road,** **Maybe you'll be a star.** **I'll take the low road and try to go real far.** **You've been my best buddy for as long as I remember.** **Remember the time I climbed a tree,** **I couldn't get down.** **You waited there so patiently till I was found.** **And the time we played hide and seek** **And you were lost nearly a week.** **How we laughed when you came home.** **You'll take the high road,**

> **Maybe you'll be a star.**
> **I'll take the low road and try to go real far.**
> **You've been my best buddy for as long as I remember.**
> **I remember. As I remember.**

(Spoken) I guess we had better leave for town now.

LIGHTS FADE AS THEY EXIT

SCENE 2

THE ROAD THROUGH TOWN: *JACK AND PENNY ENTER*

JACK:	Cow for sale! Cow for sale! Very talented cow for sale! Anybody want to buy a cow?
JILL:	(From offstage) Jack! Jack! (She enters) Jack!
JACK:	What?
JILL:	Are you Jack?
JACK:	Yes.
JILL:	Well, I got the bucket, let's get going.
JACK:	What?
JILL:	I got the bucket. The hill is over there. Let's….GO!
JACK:	Who are you?
JILL:	I'm Jill. Remember…? Jill?
JACK:	No.
JILL:	We're supposed to take this bucket and climb that hill and get a bucket of water. Remember?
JACK:	No.
JILL:	It's all here in our contract. (Removes contract from her pocket and reads.) "The Undersigned," that's us, "hereby agree to climb the hill, hereafter "Hill," and fetch one (1) pail of water." And here are our signatures, see? (Shows contract to Jack.)
JACK:	That's not my signature. You have the wrong Jack. I'm Jack Jackson, Jr.

JILL:	Jack Jackson Jr.? Didn't your father get…
PENNY:	Jill!
JILL:	Sorry.
JACK:	That's okay.
JILL:	Well, I had better go. Gotta find the right Jack (She exits.) Jack, Oh Jack! Jack! (Tarzan yell) Oh, J-a-a-a-a-a-ck!
JACK:	Strange girl! Cow for sale! Cow for sale! (Bean Man enters.)
BEAN:	Say there Boy! Am I hearing correctly? You're selling that there cow?
JACK:	Yes, sir. She's a great cow. Very talented. She can tap dance! Watch.

SONG: #3 TEA FOR TWO

PENELOPE DANCES A FEW STEPS

BEAN:	Oh, a hoofer! Well, if she's so wonderful, why are you selling her?
JACK:	Well, you see, we're real poor and..
BEAN:	Yes, yes, I understand. Things are tough all over! Have you had any offers for her?
JACK:	No sir. Not yet. But watch. Dance some more, Penelope.

PENELOPE DANCES AGAIN: THEY APPLAUD WHEN SHE FINISHES AND SHE BOWS DEEPLY.

BEAN:	Tell you what kid. Now, you're having trouble unloading that cow, and I think I know why! Not a big market for cows that dance. So, come here. Have you ever heard of' Magic Mexican beans? Of course you haven't. Well, sonny, let me tell you about these beans! Once you got 'em in your pocket, the whole world changes! You got sickness? You'll get well! Poverty plaguing you? You'll get rich (Music starts) Tell you what I'm gonna do for you, Sonny. I'm gonna make you a special deal. Limited time. Only for you! (He sings)

SONG #4: THE BEAN SONG

You see folks, I got Beans to trade.
Lotsa beans.

Little ones, big ones, round ones, flat ones,
Brown ones.
I even got pink ones!
Beans to make you see,
Beans to make you grow,
Some for your shooters,
And some that look like toes!
I got beans to trade
The likes you've never seen before.
And for you and you only
I'm gonna throw in ten extra beans!

I got lotsa beans,
But you gotta hurry, hurry while they last,
Better jump on this offer cause you won't get
Another chance!
No Siree!
You see, I got these magic beans to trade!

(Spoken) Now you take these beans and run along. (He gives the beans to Jack. Jack gives him Penelope's rope.) You have made your fortune this day!

JACK: Mister, could I say goodbye to my cow?

BEAN: Sure.

JACK: In private?

BEAN: Oh, yeah, sure. I'll just wait over here.

JACK: (They exchange the rope) Well, Penelope, it's done. I've traded you for magic beans. You understand, I've got to do what's best for my family. (Penelope shakes her head, "Yes," "No," consecutively.) All right, Mister. You can take her now.

BEAN: You won't regret this, Sonny.

JACK: I already do.

SONG # 5: BEST BUDDY REPRISE

JACK: You've been my best buddy for as long as I remember.
Remember the time I climbed a tree
And couldn't get down.
PENNY: I waited there so patiently till you were found.

     And the time we played hide and seek,
     And I was lost for nearly a week,
     How we laughed when I came home.

Both: You've been my best buddy for as long
     As I remember. I remember.
     As I remember.

LIGHTS FADE

SCENE 3

OUTSIDE JACK'S HOUSE. MOM AND THE SPRATS ARE TALKING

MOM: (Pacing and fretting) I wonder where Jack is? He's been gone all day. I hope he sold the cow. I hope he got a good price for her. I hope he didn't run away. I hope he wasn't led away like those poor children over in Hamlin.

FANNY: Wasn't that awful?

J.S.: Don't worry. Jack's fine.

SPRATS: He'll come home.

WITCH: (Enters) Who killed my sister?

ALL: What?

WITCH: Who killed my sister?

ALL: What are you talking about?

WITCH: That's my line! Look. (Takes out a script) See, right here? Witch enters. "Who killed my sister?" So, I'll try it one more time. (She exits and enters again.) Who killed my sister?

ALL: Wrong story!

WITCH: What?

ALL: Wrong story!

WITCH: Oh.

JACK: (Enters) Mom! Mom! Look what I got!

MOM: Oh, Jack! Are you all right? Did you sell the cow? Did you get a good price for her?

JACK: I'm fine. I sold the cow, and I got something better than money!

MOM: Better than money? What do you mean, Jack?

JACK: Oh, Mom, I got BEANS!

MOM: (A beat) Beans.

JACK: Magic Mexican Beans.

MOM: (A beat) Beans.

JACK: They'll make all our dreams come true!

MOM: Beans…beans. Beans.

JACK: Maaaaagic Beans!

WITCH: Oooo. Can I see? Yep! They're beans.

MOM: (Imitating Jack) I see, maaaagic Beans. And what makes them magic?

JACK: The Bean Man promised! He said I made my fortune today!

MOM: The Bean Man promised. He promised they're magic? Oh Jack, Jack, Jack. You can't trust magic! It's almost as bad as show business. You can't pin your hopes on a star!

JACK: What does that mean?

WITCH: What your mom says is true, young man. You can't really trust magic. I should know!

(She sings)

SONG #6: MAGIC

Magic is a dubious thing:
A doubtful, debatable, curious thing.
Magic is a delicate thing:
An unreliable sometimes thing.

> You can spend your time chanting rhymes
> With a wish and a dream and a prayer.
> But where will you be
> When it comes to the end
> And you don't have a dime to spare?
> Magic is a dubious thing:
> A doubtful, debatable, curious thing.
> Magic is a delicate thing:
> You can't always tell,
> And you don't always know.
> It just might turn out you have nothing to show
> In the end!

ALL: You can spend your time, etc. to end of song.

SONG ENDS

MOM: So, I don't want to hear any more about magic! Give me those beans! (She takes beans from Jack and throws them offstage.) Now, Jack, go to bed!

J.S.: Oh…um…yeah…it's getting late. Come on Fanny, let's go home.

FANNY: Oh, oh, oh. Okay.

ALL: Goodnight.

THEY ALL TURN THEIR BACKS. THE VINE GROWS. SFX

MOM: What was that?

JACK: I don't know.

WITCH: Did you hear that sound?

J.S.: Yes.

JACK: I heard it too! (Vine grows some more SFX)

FANNY: There it goes again!

JACK: Look! (They all look at the vine.)

J.S.: Yuk! A big ugly beanstalk!

FANNY: Jack!

J.S.: Well, look at it, Fanny! Who wants that big monstrous thing in their yard?

FANNY: Jack!

WITCH: Wow! Whodda thought?

MOM: He's right! Jack, get the axe!

JACK: But it's magic, Mom!

MOM: Magic my sweet patooty! Mr. Sprat is right! I won't have that ugly thing in my yard!

JACK: I've got to see where it goes! (He starts to climb the stalk.)

MOM: Jack! Get down here this instant! Do you hear me?

SONG #7: JACK, COME BACK

Jack, come back!
You didn't even ask, Jack!
Jack, come back!
You didn't even ask, Jack!
Think of all the other Jacks
Who didn't listen to their mothers.
They were in such a terrible rush.
That's why they got in so much trouble!

There was Jack the nimble one.
He was quick.
He tried to jump a candle stick.
And when Jack and Jill went up the hill,
Look what happened to them!
Little Jack Horner had to sit in the corner.
And poor Jack Sprat has such a dietary problem!

If you climb up to the sky,
Who knows what you'll find, Jack!
You might fall through a cloud,
And the thunder will be so loud up there, Jack!

Jack, come back.
You didn't even ask, Jack!
Jack, come back!

You didn't even ask, Jack!
(Repeat and fade.)

JACK CLIMBS AWAY AS THE LIGHTS FADE.

SCENE 4

GIANTLAND

JACK:	Boy, this is a spooky place! (Giant yawns offstage) What was that? (Giant snores.) I don't like the sound of that!
GIANT:	Hey! Somebody's in the house! I can smell him! Fee, fie, foe, fum…
JACK:	Yikes! I'm in trouble now!
GIANT:	(Entering) Fee, fie, foe, fum. I smell the blood of an Englishman! Be he alive or be he dead, I'll grind his bones to make my bread! (Spots Jack) There you are, you little intruder! Fee, fie, foe, fum! I smell the blood of an Englishman…
JACK:	Then there must be someone else here.
GIANT:	Huh?
JACK:	Because I'm not a man. I'm a boy.
GIANT:	Oh.
JACK:	And I'm not English. I'm second generation American.
GIANT:	Oh.
JACK:	So you see, there's no use in grinding my bones. I'd make lousy bread anyway.
GIANT:	Oh, I don't really do that. Whole wheat.
JACK:	What?
GIANT:	Whole wheat. I only eat whole wheat. It's good for you. Keeps you regular. Say, who are you? What are you doing here?
JACK:	I'm Jack Jackson, Jr.
GIANT:	Jack Jackson, Jr.? Didn't your father get scrambled…oops, sorry.
JACK:	It's all right.

GIANT: Well, what are you doing here, Jack Jackson, Jr.?

JACK: Well, you see, we're poor, I traded the cow, got the beans, Mom got mad, threw the beans, stalk grew, I climbed, I'm here.

GIANT: (Sincerely) Uh-huh, uh-huh, uh-huh! Quite a story. You seem like a nice kid, so now that you've seen what's up here, why don't you run on home? Your mama's probably very worried about you. Besides, I got work to do. (He unties a bag from his waist and empties its contents onto the table and begins to count.) Uh, one, um, two, three, um…What comes next? Oh, yeah, uh, seven…

JACK: Is that real gold?

GIANT: Yeah. Um ten, thirteen, um two…Oh, look what you did. You made me lose count! Now I have to start all over again. Um, one, two, three. Um nine…

JACK: But is it really gold?

GIANT: Yes, it's really gold! Twenty-two, seventy-twelve…Oooh! You did it again!

JACK: Is it yours?

GIANT: Yes, it's mine. Six hundred and tooty…Why?

JACK: Because my mom and I are real poor. That's why I had to sell the cow. And if I had just one piece of that gold, our lives would be a lot easier. We could buy food and we wouldn't be hungry.

GIANT: Tell you what kid. I'll give you some of this gold if you'll go away and leave me alone!

JACK: It's a deal!

GIANT: Good. Here take this and go. (He puts some gold in the bag and gives it to Jack.)

JACK: Gee, thanks! Mom is going to be so happy! This is a real nice thing you did, Mr. Giant. You have a big heart.

GIANT: Giant sized! You're a good son, Jack Jackson, Jr.! (Jack hurries down the bean stalk.) Now maybe I can get my work done! (Counts) Um…one, two, three, fifty seven…nine, tooty-five…

BLACKOUT

SCENE 5

IN FRONT OF JACK'S HOUSE

JILL: Jack, oh Jack! Jaaaaaaack!

WITCH: Have a nice pretty apple my dear?

JILL: Have you seen Jack?

WITCH: What?

JILL: Have you seen Jack, old woman?

WITCH: (Correcting her) Witch.

JILL: What?

WITCH: Witch

JILL: What witch?

WITCH: Me.

JILL: What?

WITCH: Witch

JILL: What?

WITCH: What?

JILL: Where's Jack?

WITCH: Who?

JILL: Jack!

WITCH: Which Jack?

JILL: Jack's a witch?

WITCH: What!

JILL: Which?

WITCH:	Who?
JILL:	What? (Pause)
WITCH:	Have a nice pretty apple my dear?
JILL:	I'm not starting that again! (She starts to exit.)
WITCH:	Wait!
JILL:	Why?
WITCH:	What?
JILL:	Aaaaaaarrrrrgggggghhhh! (She exits.)
WITCH:	Whew! (She exits as Jack comes down the stalk.)
JACK:	Mom! Mom! Mom!
MOM:	(Enters.) Jack you're back! I was so worried!
JACK:	Look what I've got! (Hands her the sack of gold.)
MOM:	What is it? (Looking in sack) Well! Snap my garters! Jack, it's gold! Hey Sprats! Look! Gold! (Sprats enter)
FANNY:	Where did you get it Jack?
J.S.:	Yeah, where did you get it?
MOM:	Yes, Jack, where did you get it?
JACK:	From the giant who lives at the top of the beanstalk.
SPRATS:	Uh-oh!
MOM:	A giant?
JACK:	Yeah.
MOM:	Who lives at the top of the beanstalk.
JACK:	Yeah.
SPRATS:	Here it comes!
MOM:	Really, Jack! That's the most fantastic story you have ever told! I hope you didn't steal that gold!

WITCH: (Entering) Mirror, mirror, on the wall…

All: Wrong story!

WITCH: Not again!

JILL: (Enters and sees witch) Oh no! Not you!

WITCH: What?

JACK: Jill!

JILL: Jack!

JACK: Did you find Jack?

JILL: Not yet.

MOM: Jack, who is this girl? Never mind! I have bigger things to worry about! I've got to find a way to save this family!

JILL: I've got to find Jack!

WITCH: I've got to find the right story!

SPRATS: We've got to find a quieter place to live!

JACK: I've got to find some way to convince my Mom! I'm going back up that beanstalk. I'll find a way to convince everyone I'm telling the truth.

JACK CLIMBS BEANSTALK. GENERAL HUBBUB FROM EVERYONE ELSE.

BLACKOUT

SCENE 6

GIANTLAND AND JACK'S HOUSE

JACK: Hello! Mr. Giant? Are you home?

GIANT: (Entering) Hi, Jack. What's up?

JACK: I gave my mom the gold.

GIANT: That's nice.

JACK: But she didn't believe you gave it to me. She thinks I stole it! She doesn't even believe you exist!

GIANT: That's a shame.

JACK: So now I need something to prove to her that I was telling the truth.

GIANT: Maybe if you brought her something back from here—something that could only come from a giant—she would believe you.

JACK: That might work.

GIANT: Now, what have we got around here that would do the trick? I know! The hen that lays the golden eggs! That ought to do it.

JACK: I don't know. Eggs aren't really appreciated in my house, but I'll give it a try.

GIANT: Good. (Calling) Youngman! Youngman, come here please. Don't worry Jack. You won't have to keep it. Just show your mom what it does and then return it. Besides, the eggs aren't really gold. That's just their color. Inside they are just like any other egg. Only bigger. (Chicken enters.) Well, here she is. Youngman, the Hen. When you want her to lay, just say, "Youngman, lay an egg!" and she will. Of course, she also tells a bad joke when she does. Watch. Youngman, lay an egg.

HEN: (Clucking) Take my wife, please! (lays an egg.)

JACK: I see what you mean about the jokes!

GIANT: Right? Well, you better hurry along and settle this thing with your mom.

JACK: Okay, Thanks.

GIANT: You take good care of her, Jack. And bring her back as soon as you can. See you later! (Jack and the Hen climb down the beanstalk.)

JACK: Mom! Mom! Mom! Mom!

MOM: What is it now? (Sees hen.) What in the name of Colonel Sanders is that?

JACK: The giant gave it to me! This is Youngman the Hen that lays the golden eggs! Watch! Youngman, lay an egg!

HEN: A bum came up to me the other day and said he hadn't had a bite in three days. So I bit him! (Lays an egg.)

MOM: You know how I feel about eggs, Jack! Get that thing out of here! (She exits.)

HEN: Wait! Wait! I got one more. Aaarrrghh. How about a song?

JACK: Rats! Nice try. Come on Youngman, let's go back to Giantland.

THEY CLIMB THE BEANSTALK

BLACKOUT

GIANT: Did it work?

JACK: No. She wouldn't even discuss it. Do you have anything else?

GIANT: I've got it! Harpy!

JACK: What's a Harpy?

GIANT: Harpy is a singing harp. Harpy! Harpy! (Harpy enters.) Harpy, sing!

HARPY: **SONG #8: HARPY'S SONG**

**I can sing you any song you like,
La-la-la-la-la-la-la-la
La-la-la-la-la-la-la.
Songs of love or maybe songs of life,
La.......
If it's a melody you long to hear
Give me a moment to delight your ear.
I can sing you any song you like.
Just give me a chance to be brilliant,
Charming, totally disarming!
La......**
(Giant claps and the singing stops)

GIANT: Isn't she great? She knows every song ever written and you don't even have to put a quarter in her! All you have to do is say "sing," (She does, he claps) and she sings. (She does, he claps.) She'll sing all day if you tell her to sing. (She does, he claps.)

Jack, you must be careful. You might not think so, but the word s…the "s" word comes up very often in conversation. Please take it. Enjoy the singing! (Harpy sings.)

JACK: I'll take it! This will PROVE my story is true!

GIANT: Okay. See you later.

BLACKOUT

SCENE 7

JACK'S HOUSE

JACK: (Running in) Mom! Mom! Mom! (Mom and Sprats enter.)

MOM: What is that thing?

JACK: It's a magic harp!

SPRATS: Oh no! Not again!

JACK: But it is magic! Listen. Harp, sing! (She does)

MOM: Jack, I don't know where you got this thing, but make it stop! (Jack claps, she stops.)

FANNY: That's terrible! Please don't sing! (Harpy does. Jack claps.)

J.S.: (To Fanny) Even you aren't that bad when you sing! (She sings. Jack claps.)

JACK: You can't say… "that word" in front of her. Every time you say "that word," she starts "that wording!"

All: Ohhhhh!

JILL: (From offstage) Oh Jack! Jack! Jaaaaaackkkkk! (She enters) Oh hi, Jack! What was that singing? (Harpy sings. Jack claps and she stops.)

MOM: That thing is obnoxious, Jack. Get rid of it. And who is this girl?

JACK: This is Jill. We met in town. Jill, this is my mom and these are the Sprats.

FANNY: What did you say your name was?

JILL: What?

J.S.: Witch!

JILL: Not again!

J.S.: No. Look! (Pointing.) A witch!

WITCH: Come into my gingerbread house children!

ALL: Wrong story!

WITCH: That's it! I quit! No more! I get a call this morning from the Witches' Union telling me to come down here for this gig. They send me here and I try every witch part I know and they're all wrong! What gives?

ALL: There's no witch in this story!

WITCH: What?

ALL: No witch!

WITCH: What witch?

JILL: Noooooo! I can't stand it! I'm getting out of here! I have to find Jack! Oh, Jaaaaaccckkk!

JACK: Could you do me a favor, Jill?

JILL: What?

WITCH: Witch!

JILL: Anything to get away from her!

JACK: Could you return Harpy to the Giant? Just take her to the top of the Beanstalk. Okay?

JILL: Sure, no problem. (Jill and Harpy climb beanstalk). As long as she doesn't start singing! (Harpy sings, Jill screams. They exit. The Bean Man enters.)

BEAN: Oh Sonny! Sonny Boy! Hold up there a minute kid! I've been looking for you.

MOM: I'm afraid to ask. Who is this, Jack?

JACK: The Bean Man.

MOM: The Bean Man.

JACK: You know, "The Man With the Beans."

BEAN: Yes, madam. I am L.L., the Bean Man. "The Man With the Beans." My card. (He hands her a card. She reads)

MOM: "L.L. The Bean Man. The Man With the Beans." Of course.

BEAN: Yes, madam. I traded some magic Mexican beans for your son's cow. That is why I'm here. (To Jack) I must return your cow, son. She has been very unhappy without you.

JACK: But we don't have the beans anymore.

BEAN: I understand. I gotta return her anyway. I just can't stand to see a grown cow cry.

JACK: Poor Penelope. Where is she?

BEAN: Right across the lane. I'll go get her. We'll be back in a jiffy. (He exits.)

MOM: Jack, I still have one question. Where did you get the gold?

GIANT: (He either can speak from off-stage or come down the beanstalk.) I gave it to him!

MOM: (She looks around. Jack points skyward. She looks up.) GAVE it to him? And WHO might you be who GAVE it to him?

GIANT: I'm the Giant!

MOM: I see…the Giant. (She looks at Jack. He nods in agreement. She swoons. The witch and Jack catch her. She recovers enough to say,) A generous Giant?

GIANT: You could say that.

MOM: Well, snap my garters. I'll be. I'm Jack's mom, Jacklyn Jackson. (She waves up at him.)

GIANT: Nice to meet you, Mrs. Jackson. Sorry to hear about your husband.

All: Shhhhh…

GIANT: Sorry.

MOM: That's all right. Thanks for the gold, Mr. Giant.

GIANT: De nada.

MOM: I'm sorry I didn't believe you, Jack.

JACK: That's okay, Mom.

BEAN: (Entering with Penny) Look who's here!

JACK: Penny!

PENNY: Jack!

J.S.:	The cow talks?
FANNY:	Jack, pack. We're moving!
JACK:	Oh Penny, I have a lot to tell you. So much has happened.
PENNY:	I have a lot to tell you too, Jack. I missed you so much.
JACK:	But now we're back together!
MOM:	Thank you, L.L. You've made my son happy again. He has his cow back…AND we have enough money! (She jingles the money bag.) It's been a very good day.
BEAN:	It has. And you're very welcome.

SONG #9: BEST BUDDY REPRISE

MOM: **Looks like we'll see brighter days.**

JACK: **Sure glad that you get to stay.**

WITCH: **It's not all magic, despite what you have seen.**

BEAN: **A dash of something, a pocket full of beans!**

JACK & COW: You'll be my best buddy for as long as I'll remember.

ALL: **We'll remember. We will remember.**

JACK AND PENNY HUG. BLACKOUT. MUSIC BEGINS FOR FINALE/BOWS

ALL SING: **SONG #10: FEE FEE, FIE FIE, FOE FOE, FUM**

Fee, Fee, Fie, Fie, Foe, Foe, Fum
This was old Jack's tale, now we're done.
We've sung, oooh. We're done.

Fee, fee, fie, fie, foe, fum
Fee, fee, fie, fie, foe, fum

That's our story. That's our tale.
Hope you liked it cause we'd
Hate to fail.

And when we finish this song.
We'll be moving along.

Fee, fee, fie, fie, foe, fum
Fee, fee, fie, fie, foe, fum
Fee, fee, fie, fie, fie, foe, fum

THE END

MUSIC FROM
FEE, FIE, FOE, FUM...JACK'S TALE

Artwork by Christine Boyka Kluge

Book by Bill Wheeler and Jan Callner

Music and Lyrics by Jan Callner

Copyright 2006, 2013, 2025

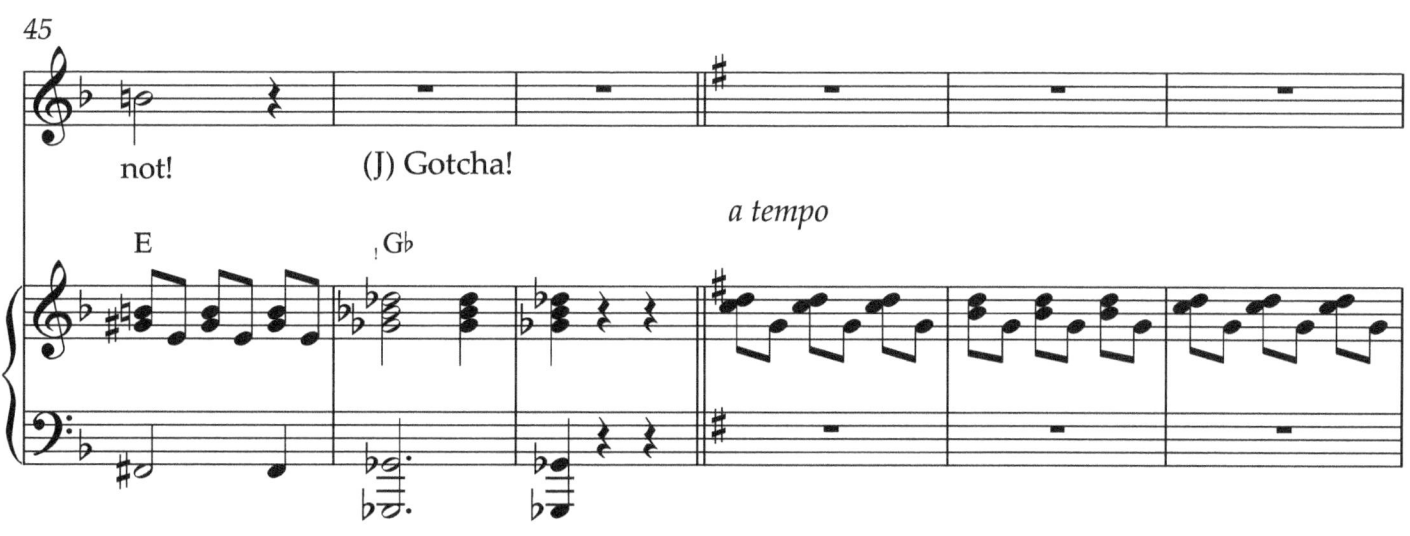
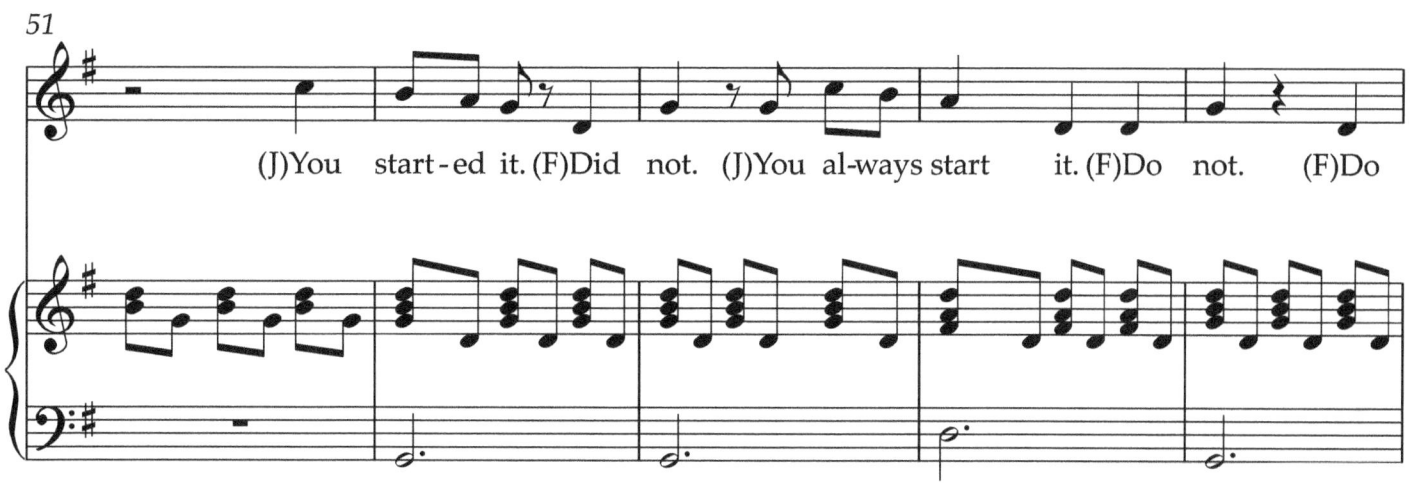

You Started It!

You Started It!

Best Buddy

Words and Music by
Jan Callner

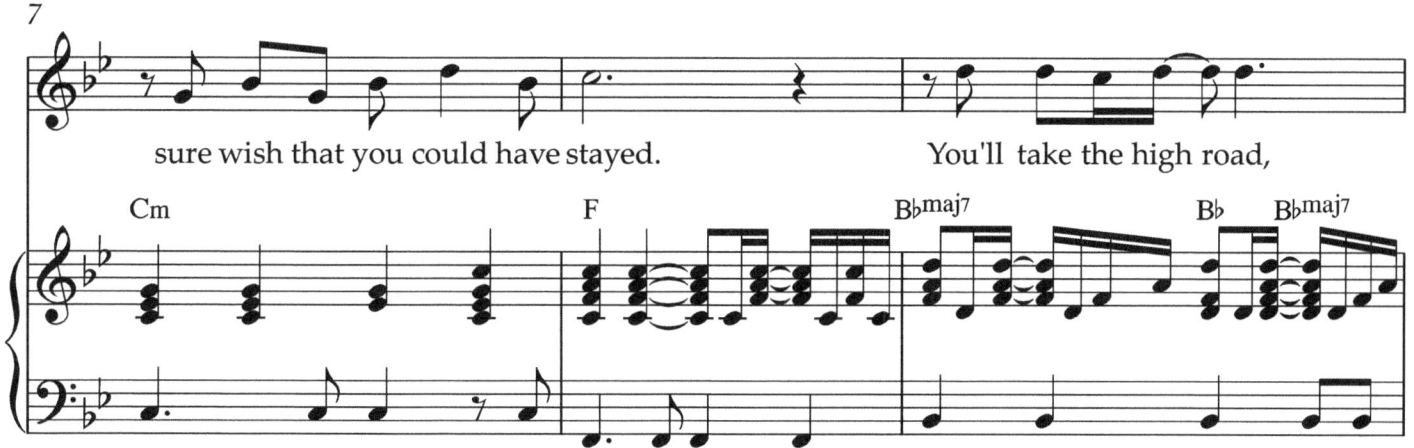

Copyright 2013 Jan Callner

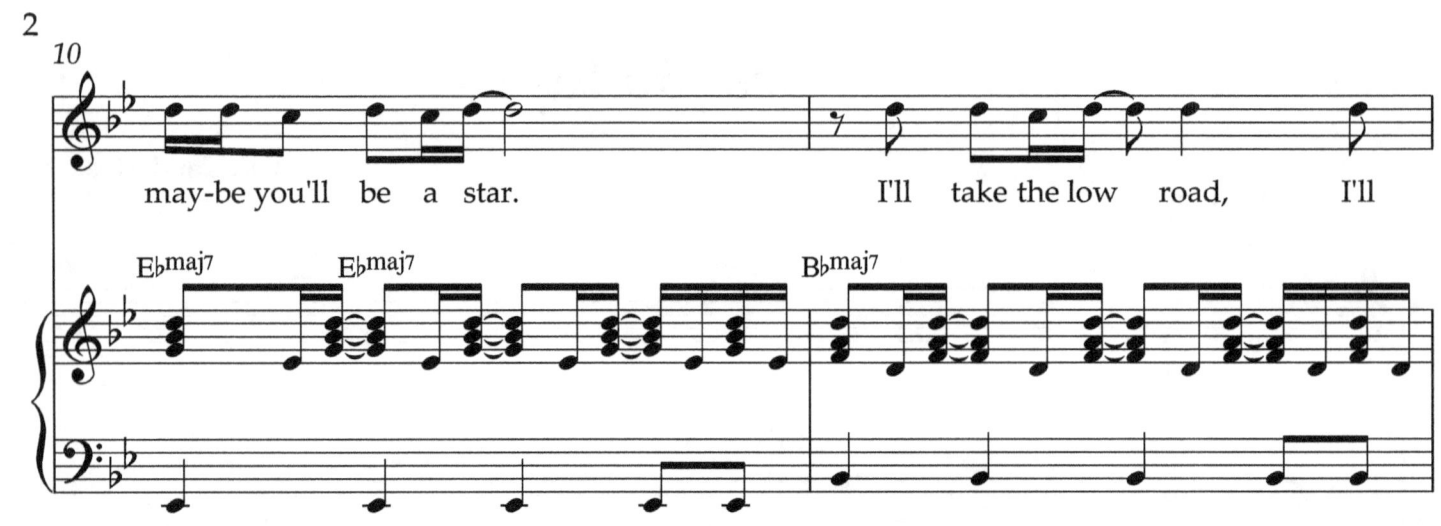

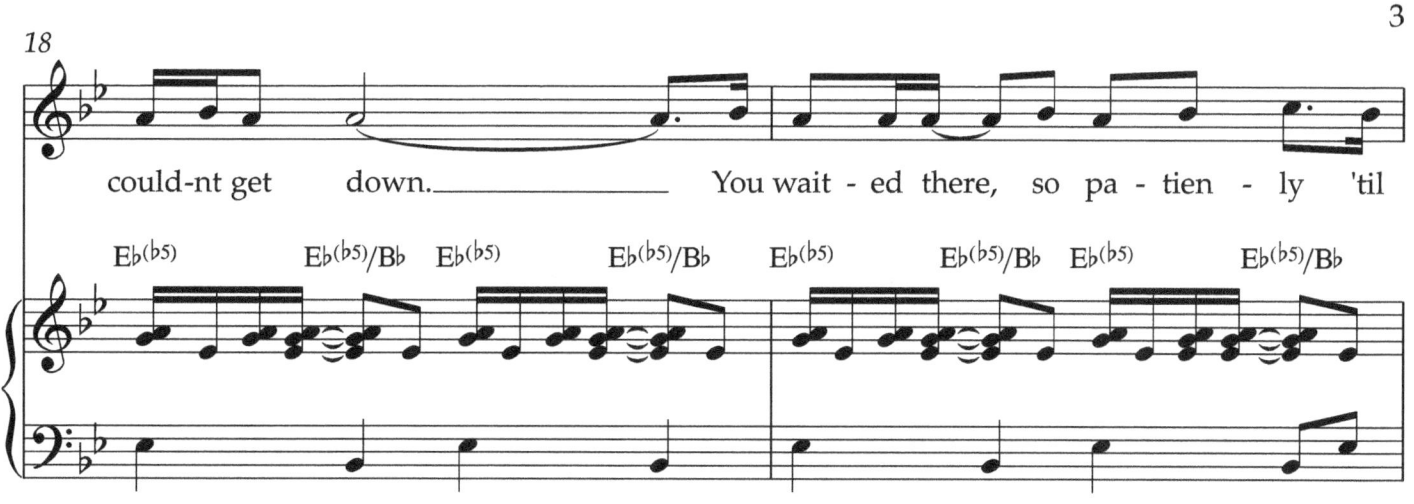

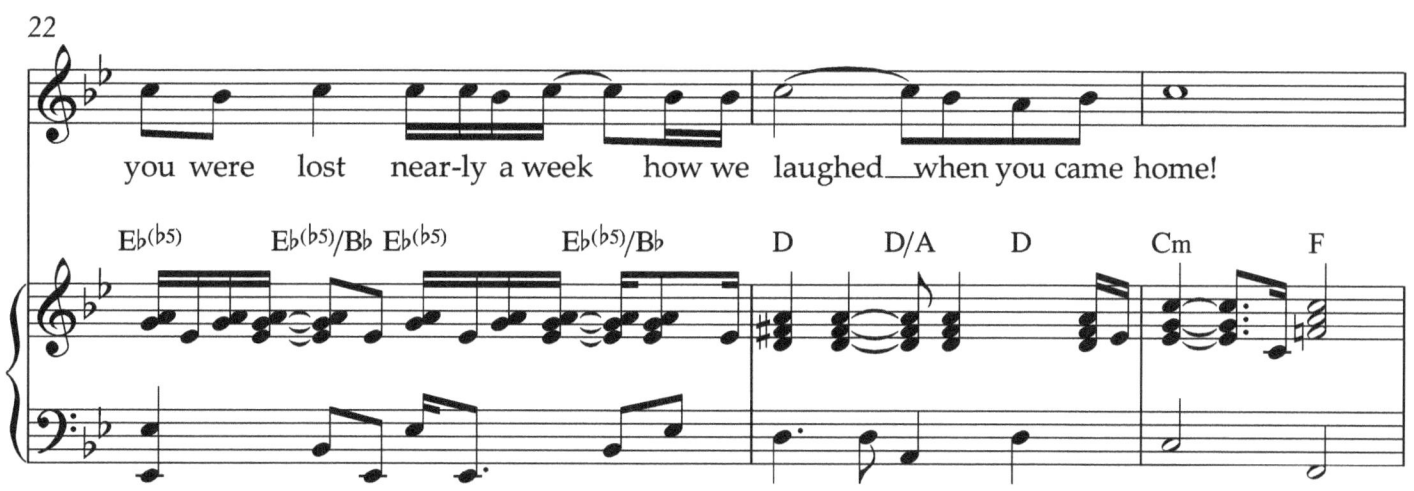

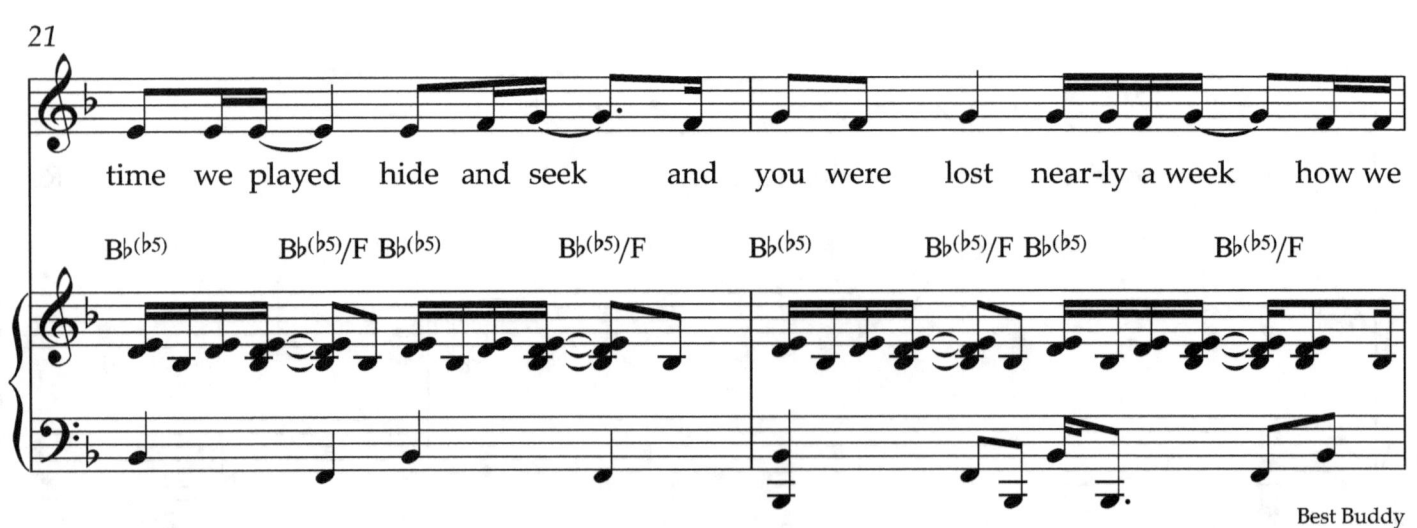

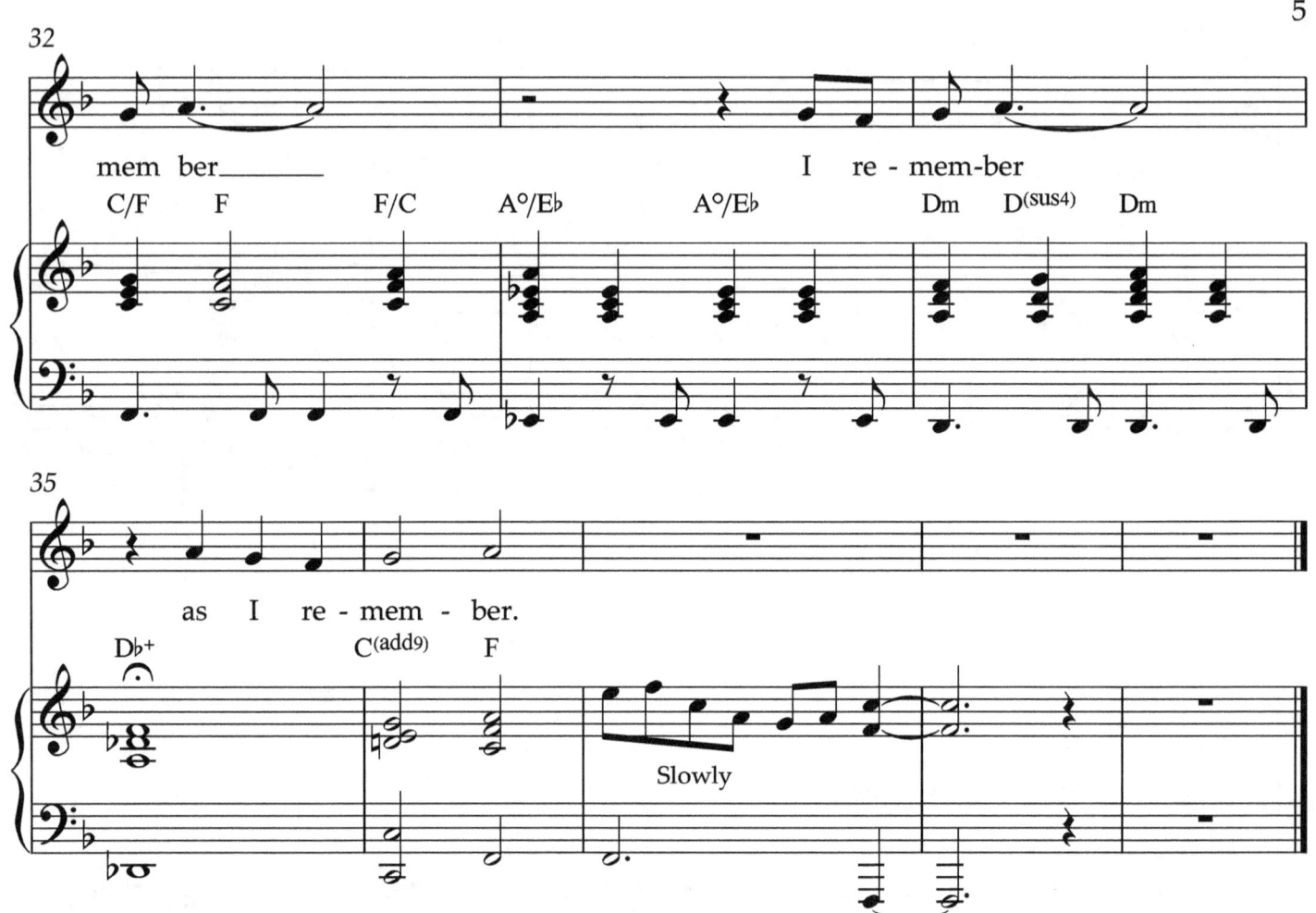

Tea for Two
A Softshoe

Vincent Youmans
arr. Henry Levine/Jan Callner

arrangement Copyright © 2025 by Jan Callner

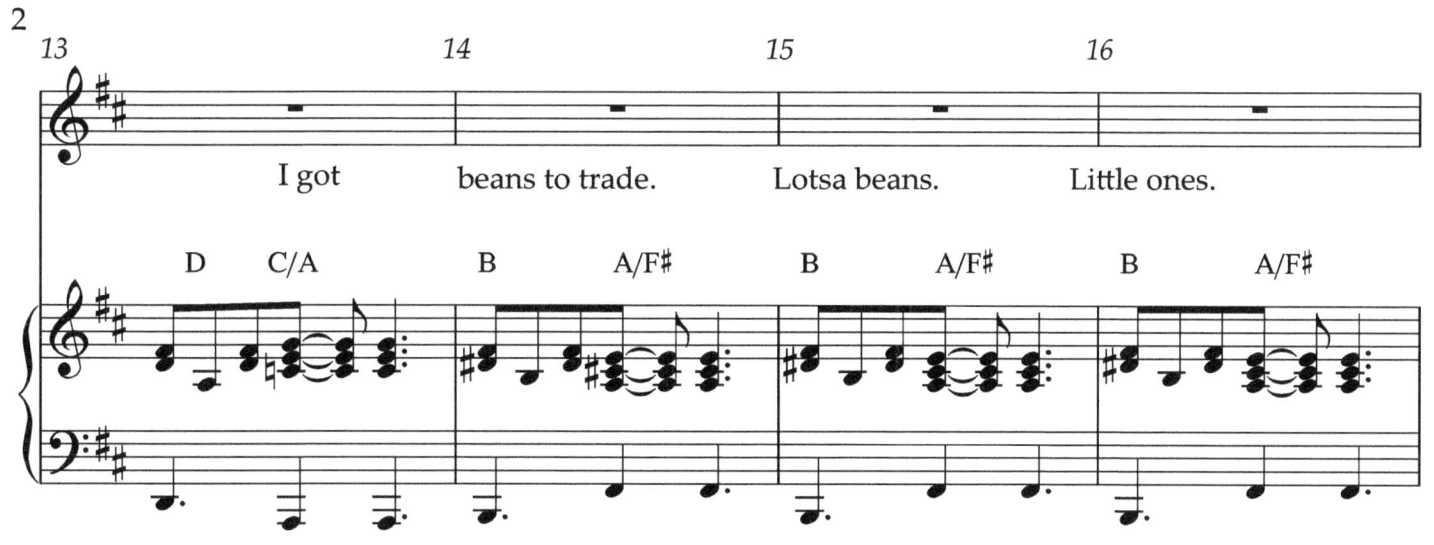
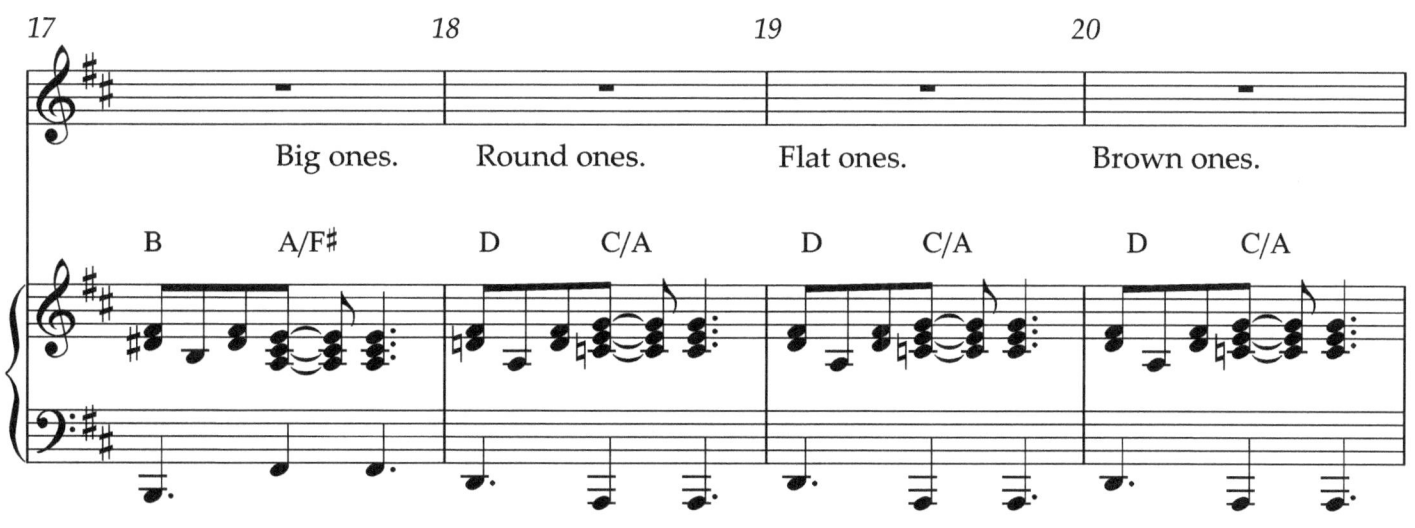

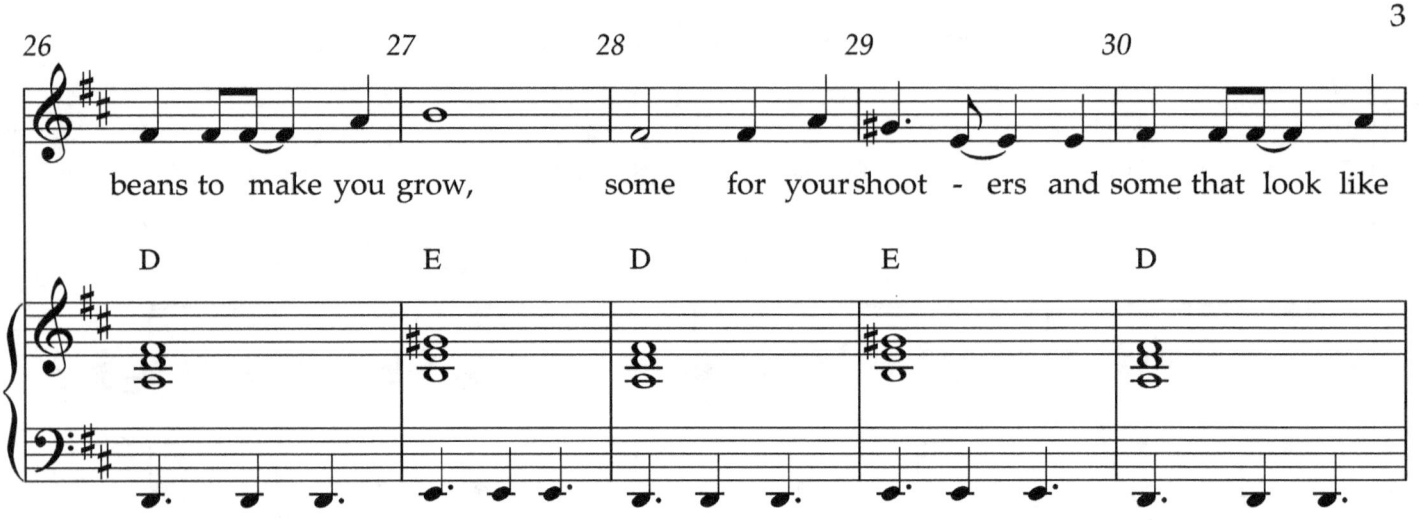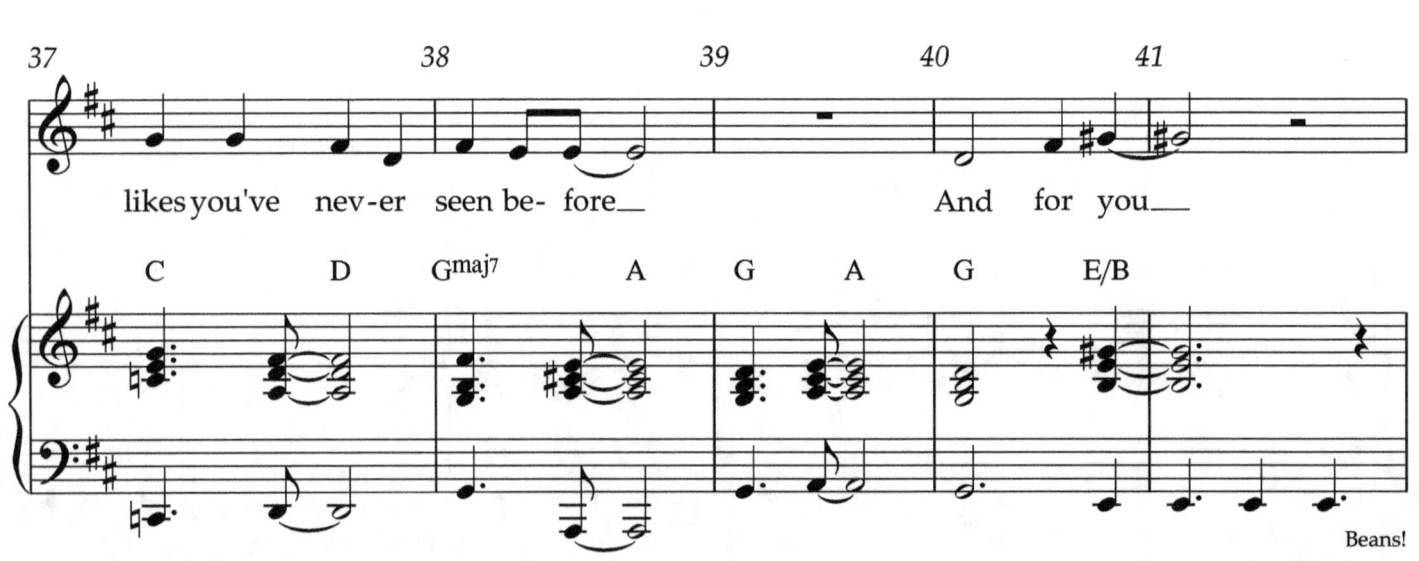

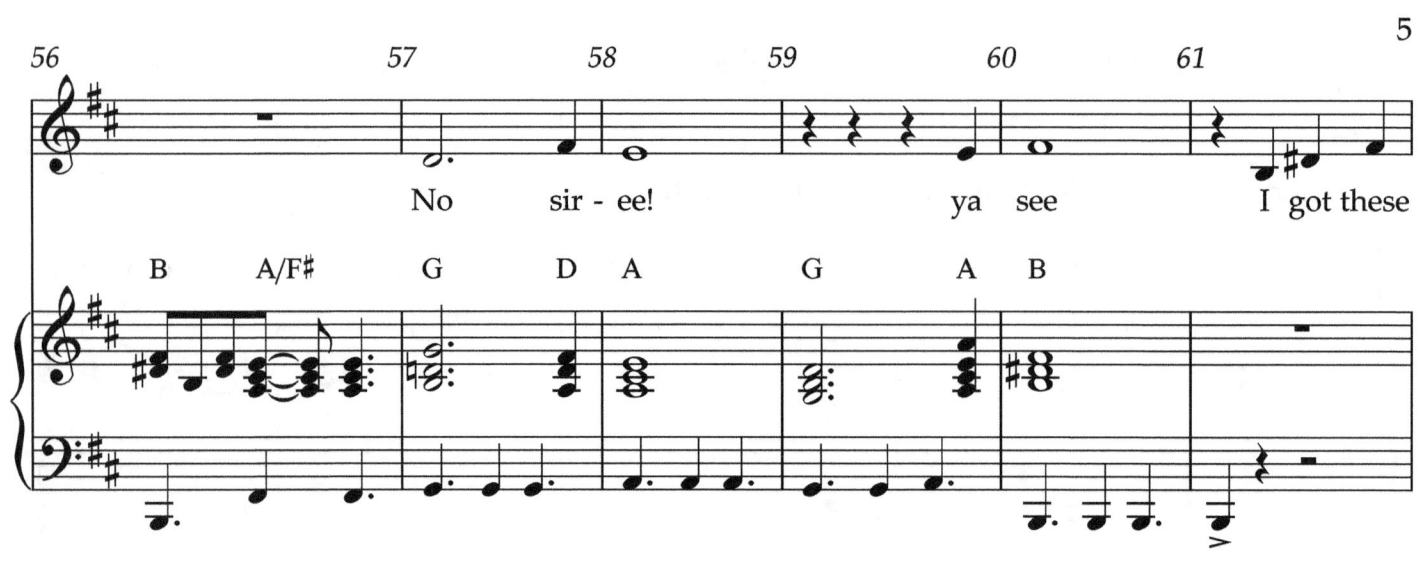
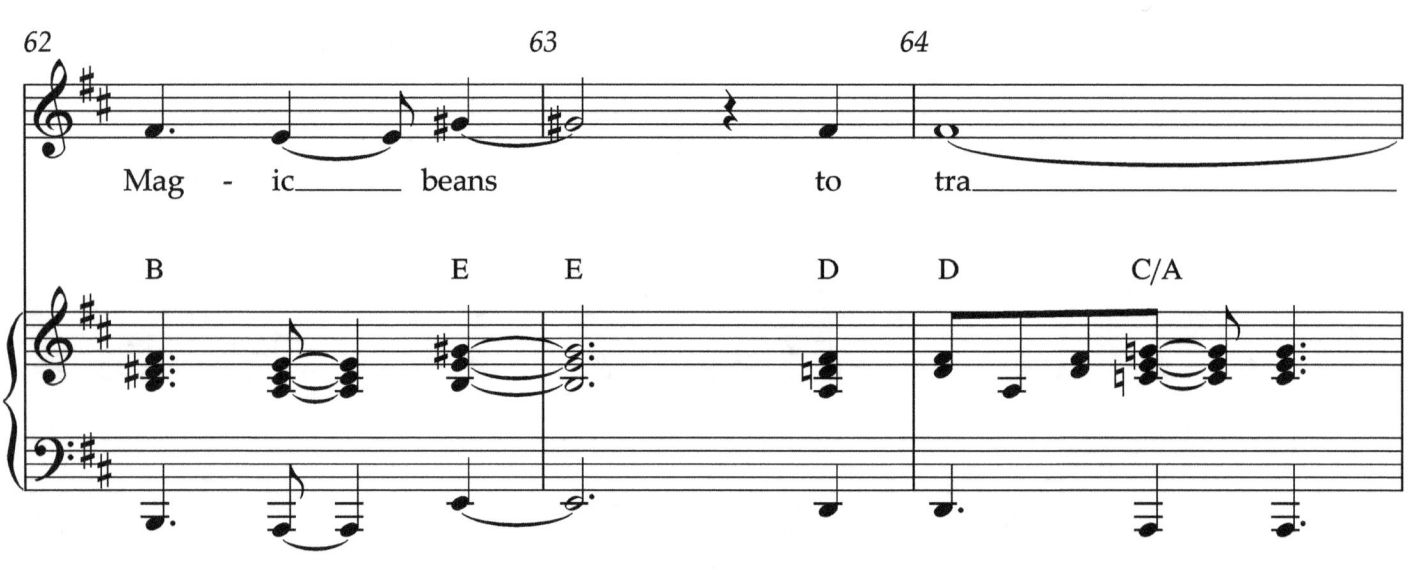
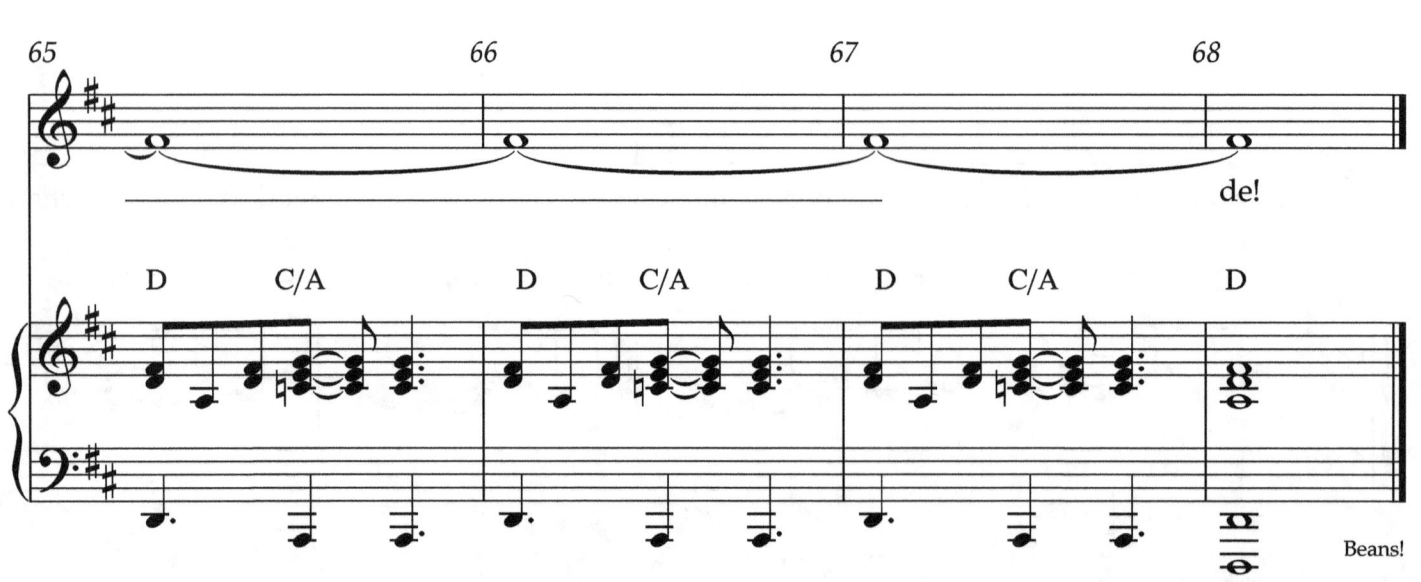

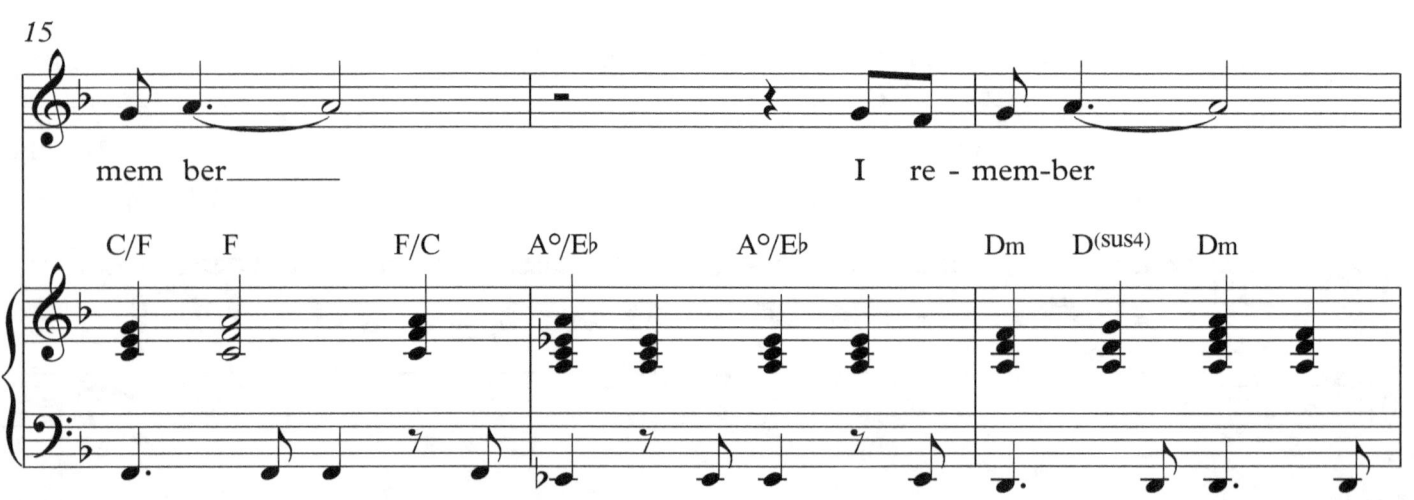

Best Buddy

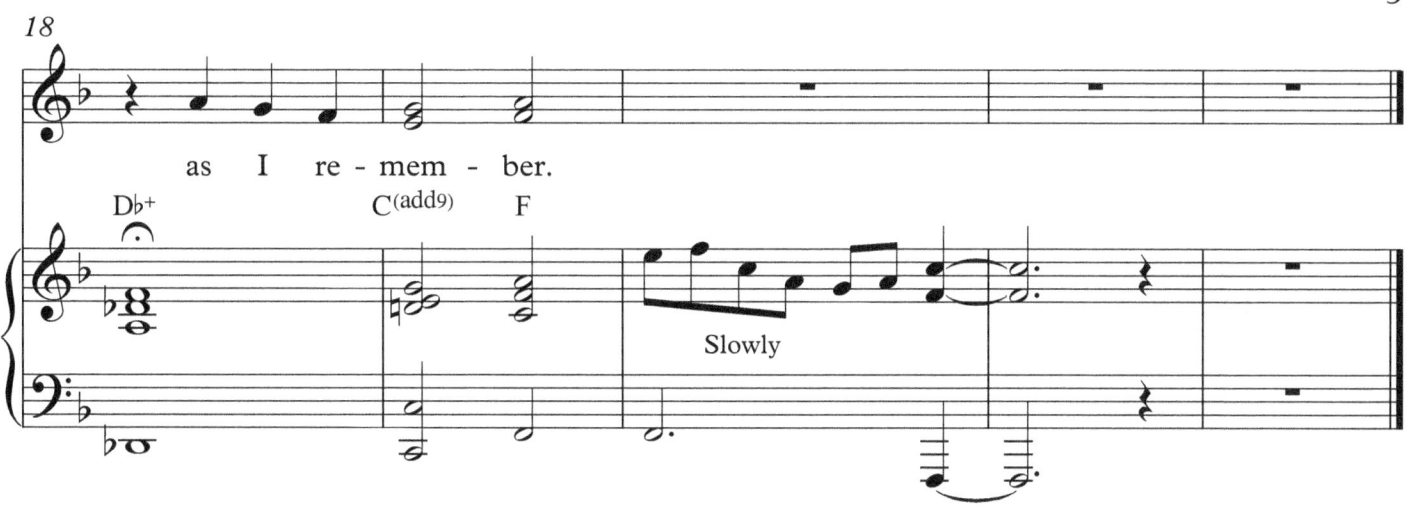

Magic

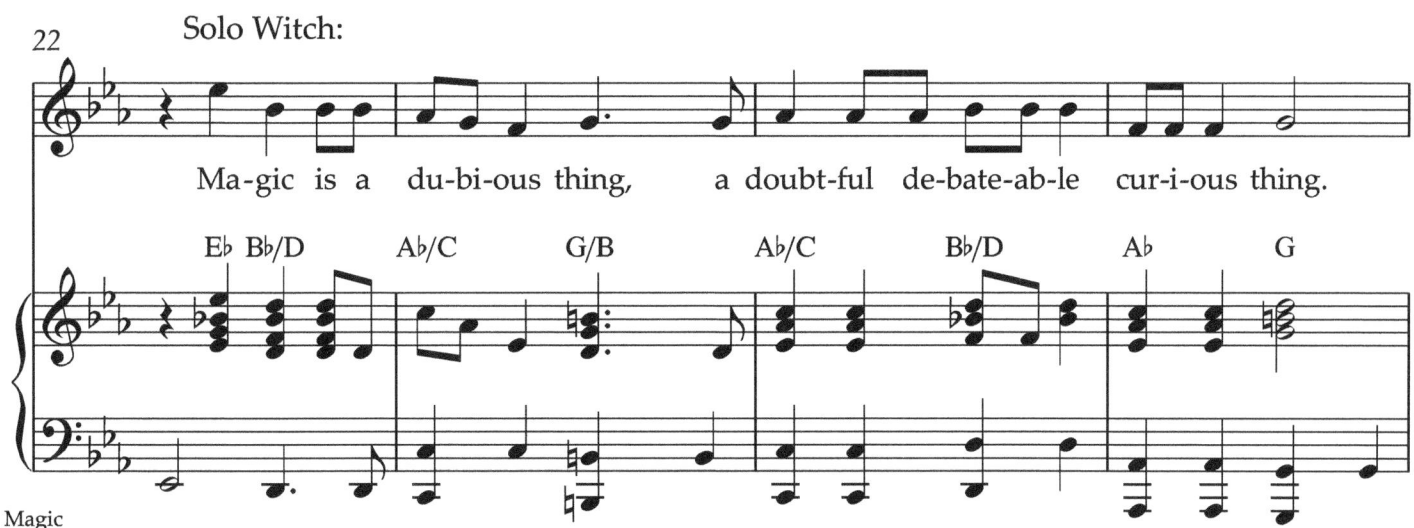

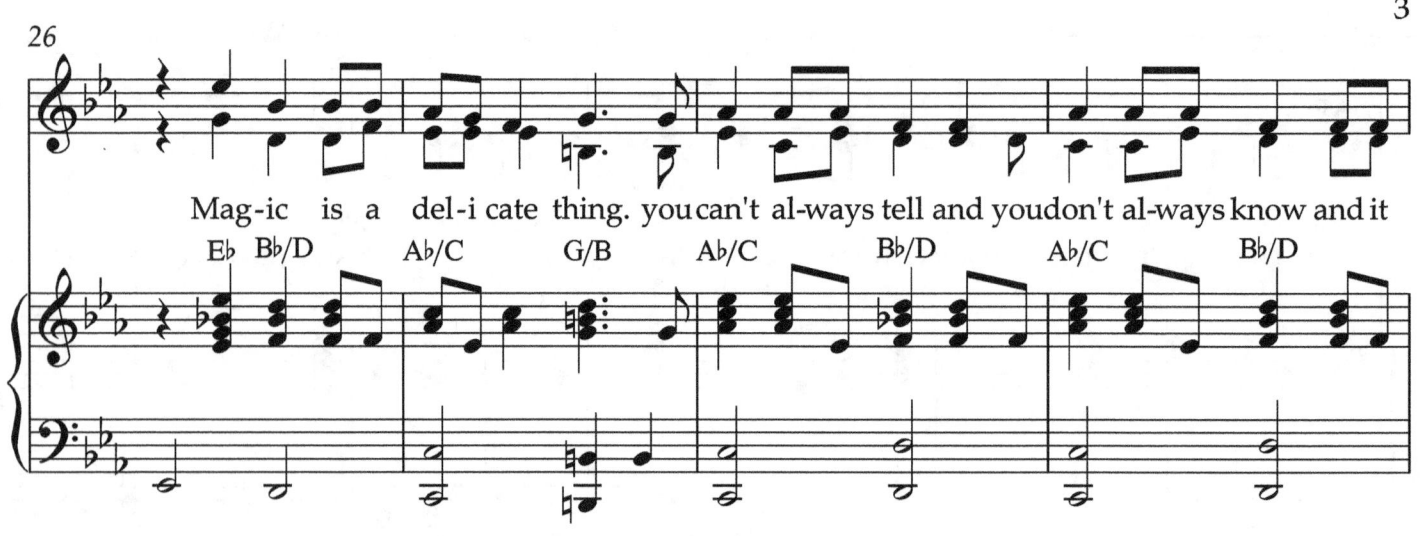
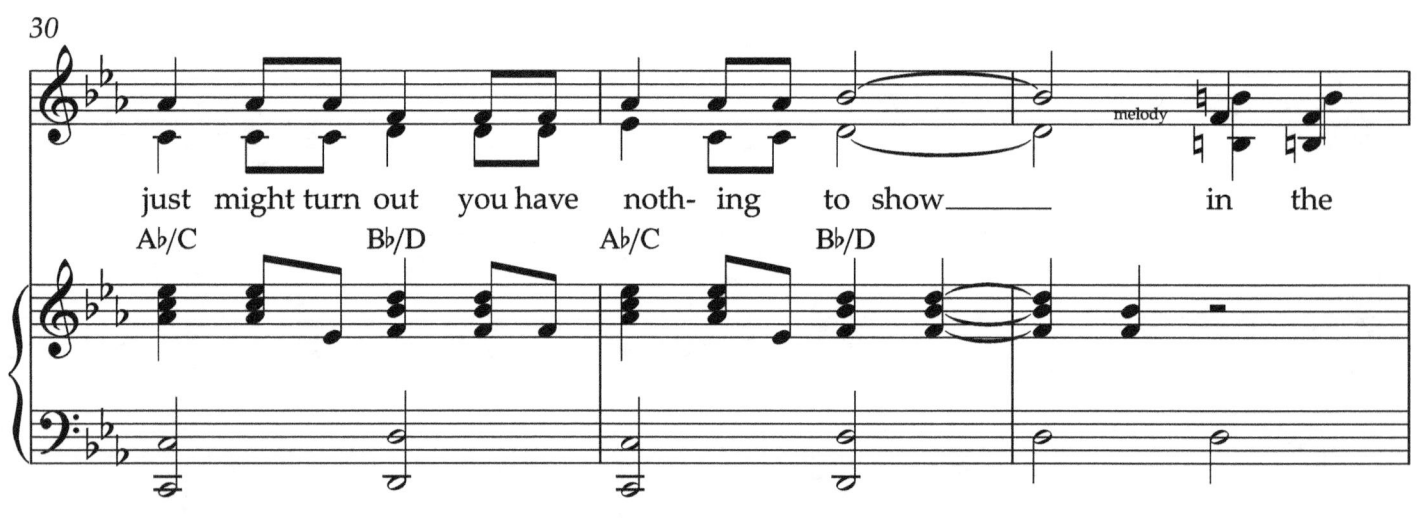
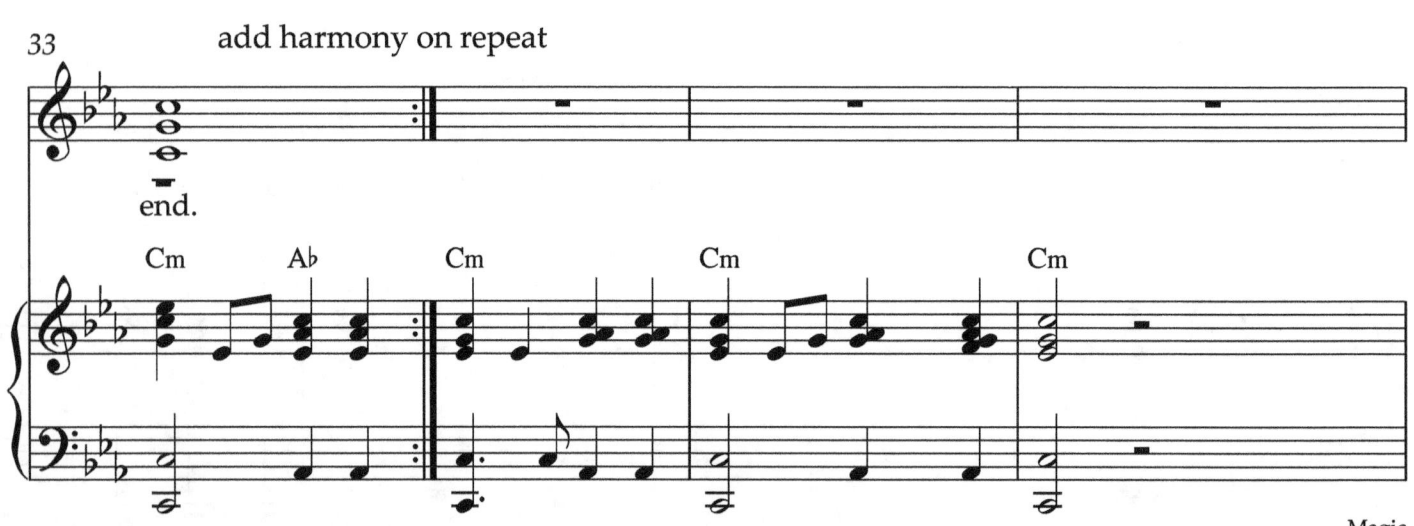

JACK...

Jack, Come Back!

Words and Music by
Jan Callner

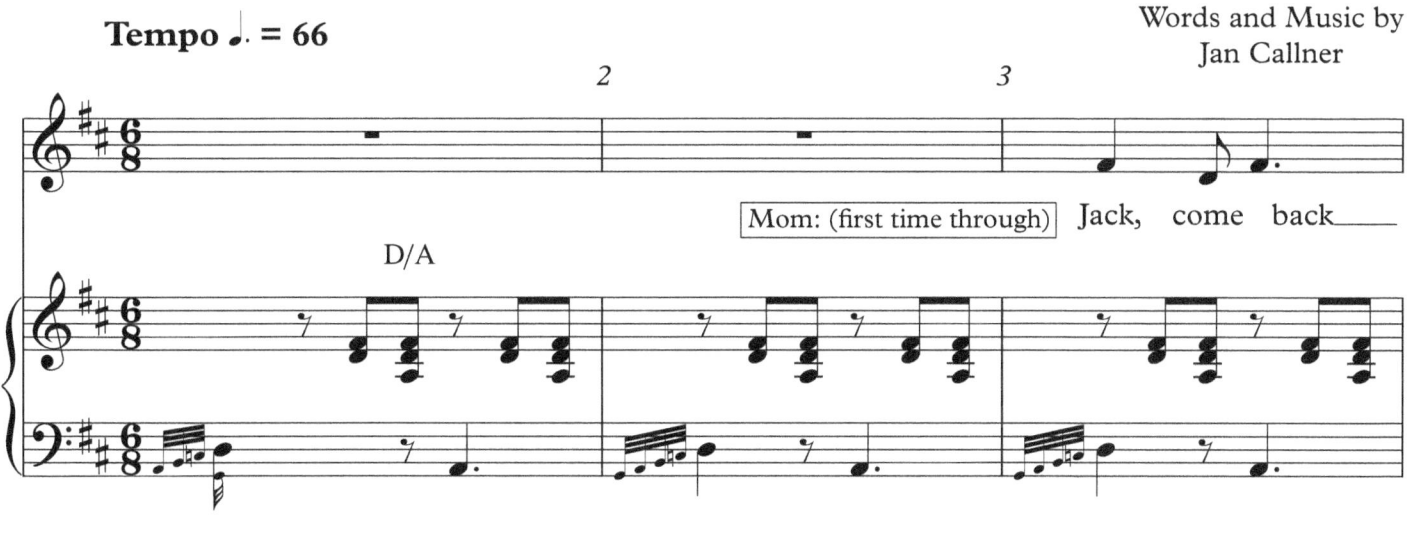

Copyright 2013 Jan Callner

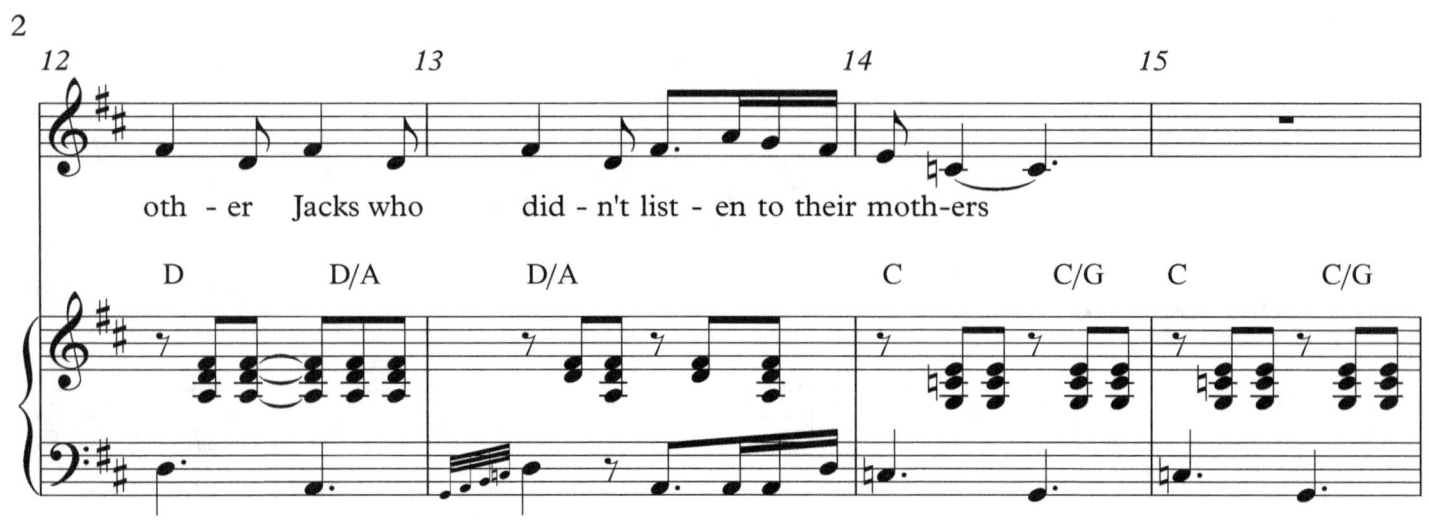

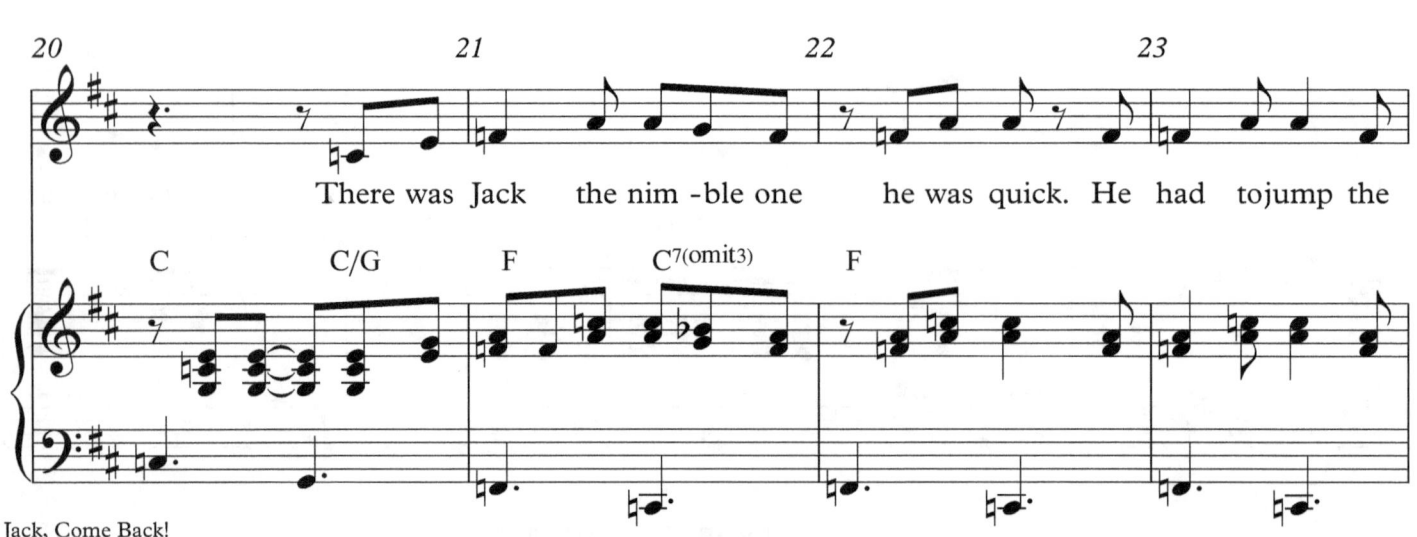

Jack, Come Back!

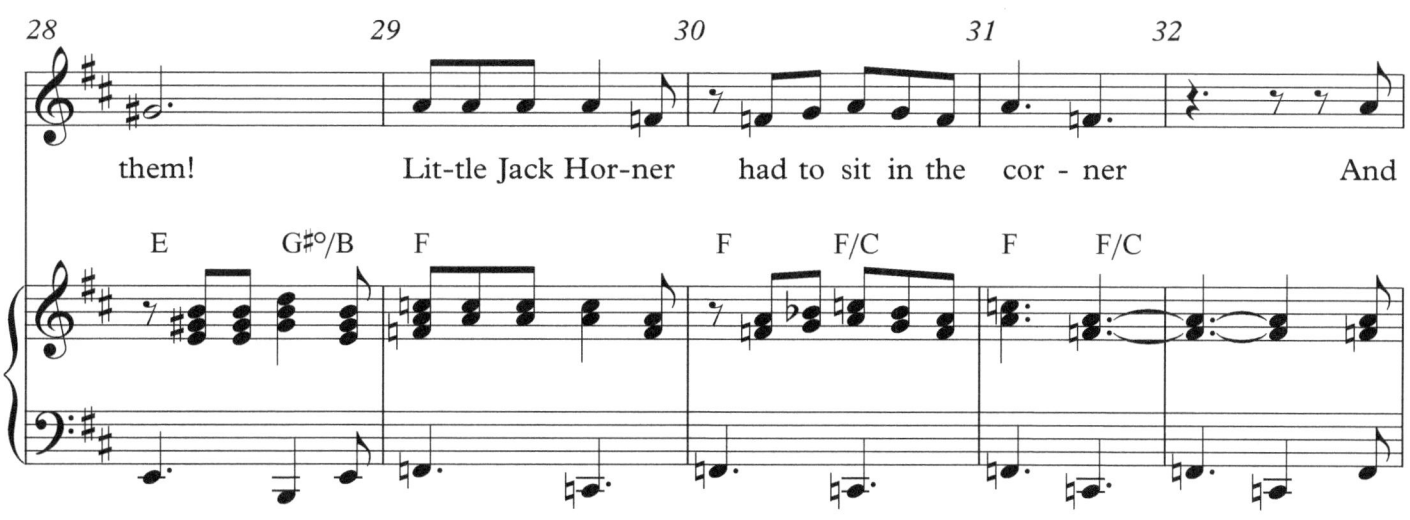
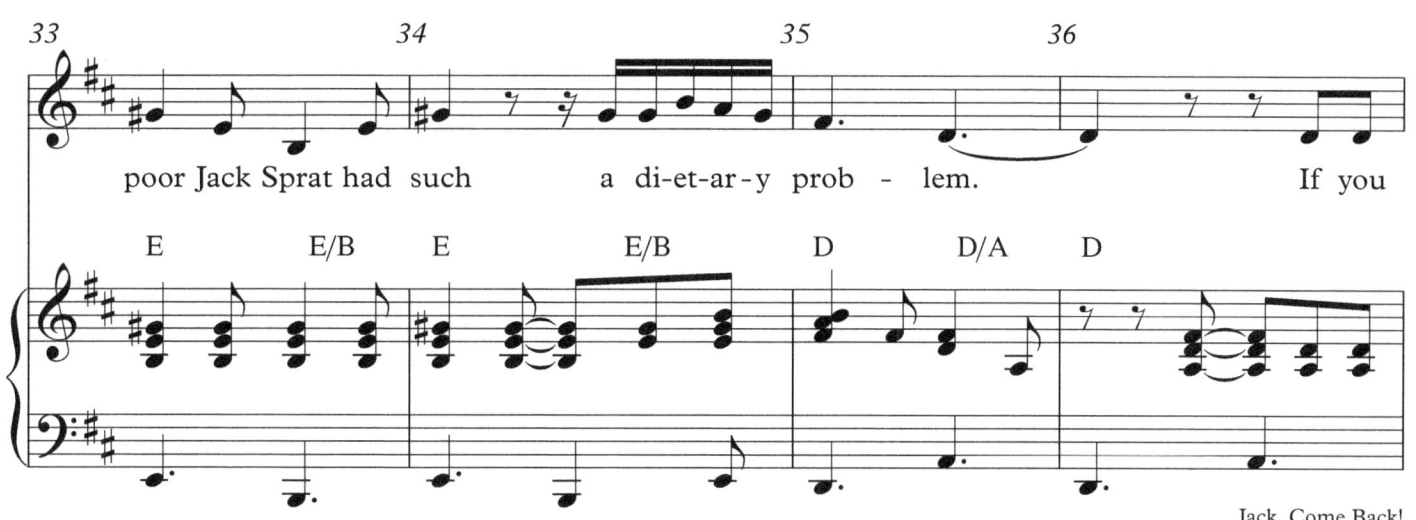

Jack, Come Back!

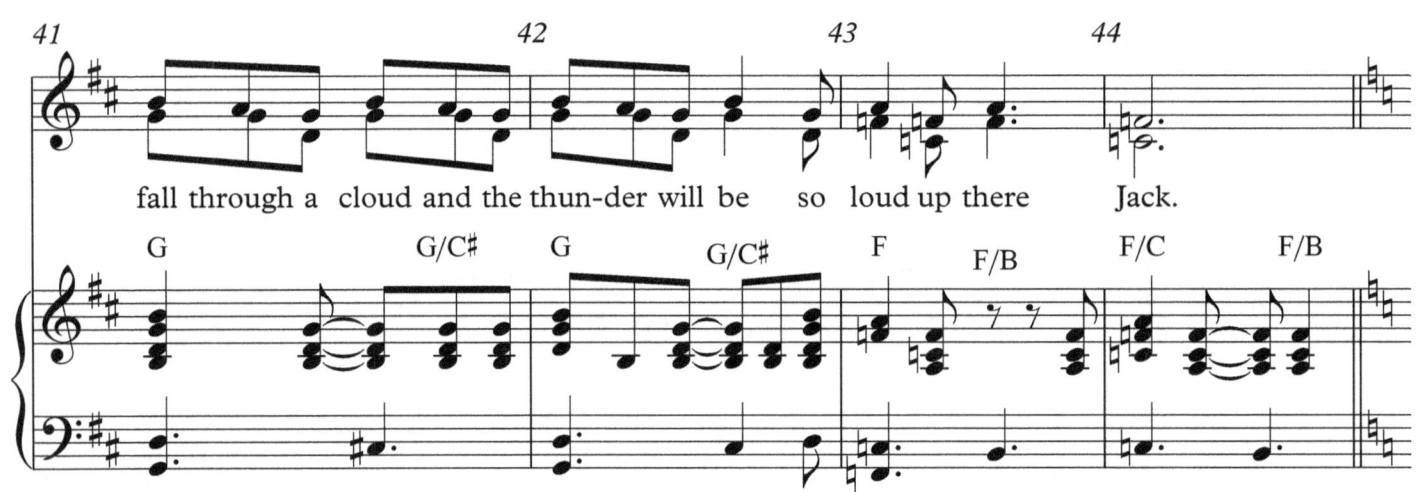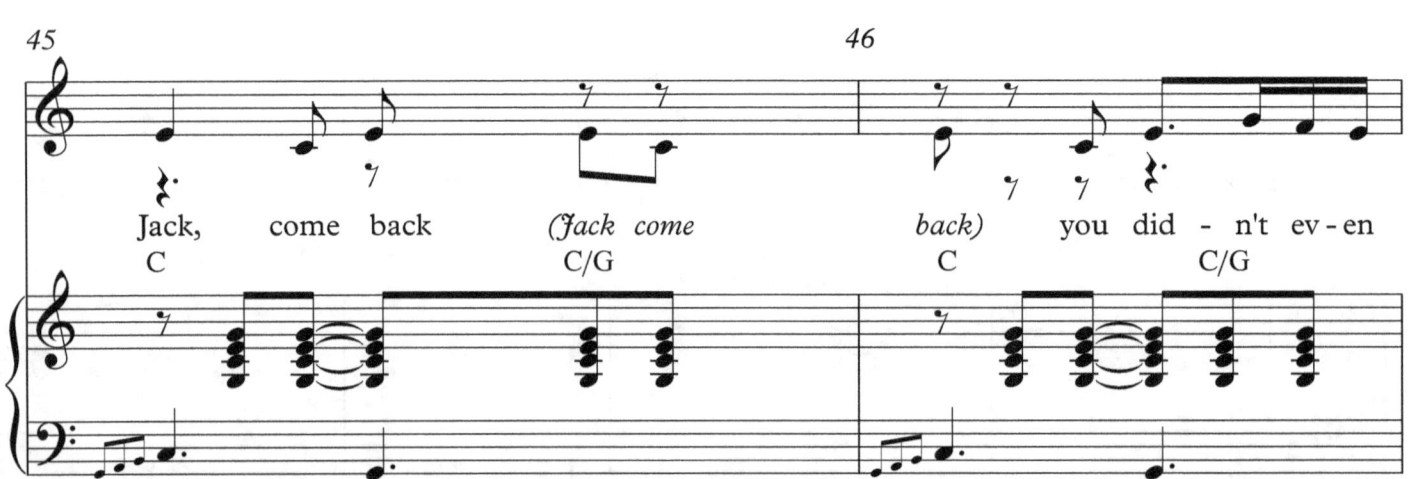

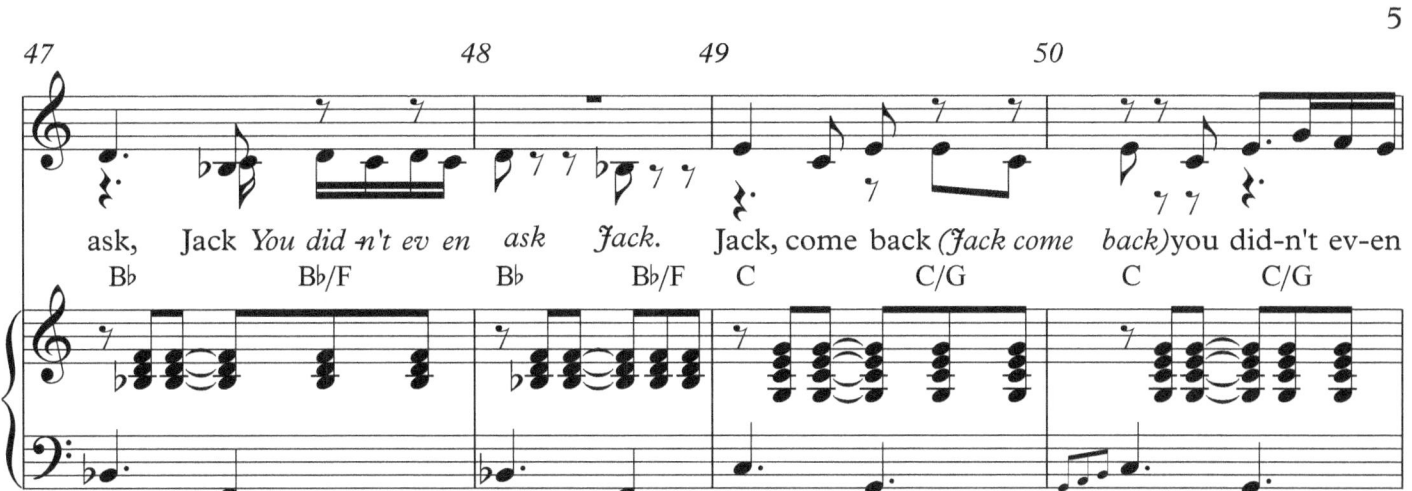

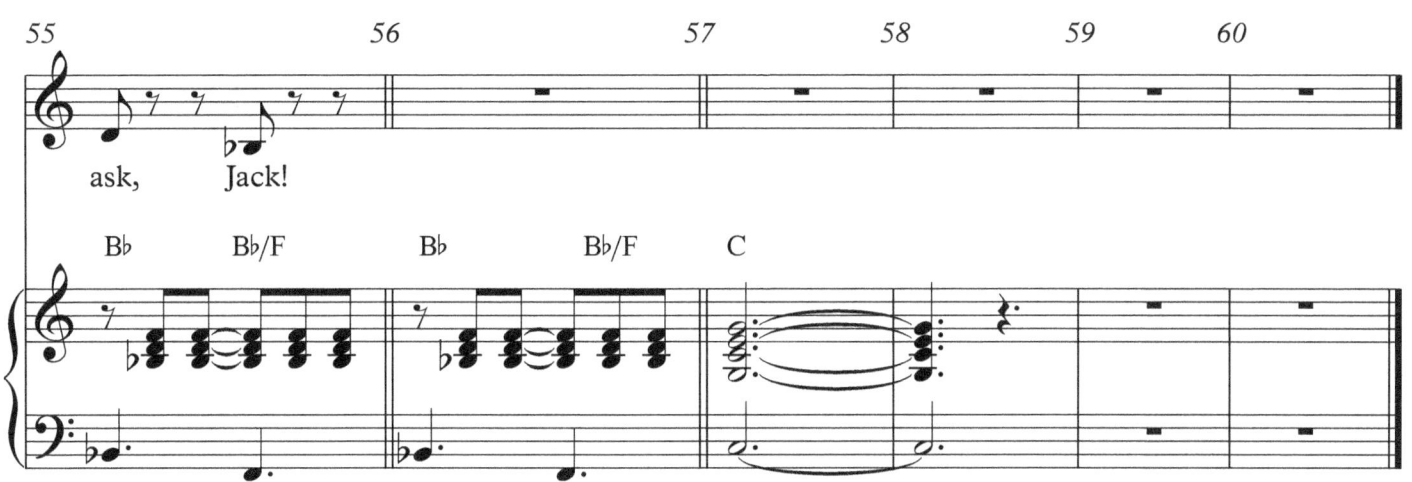

I Can Sing
(la la la la)

Words and Music by Jan Callner

Obnoxiously! ♩=160

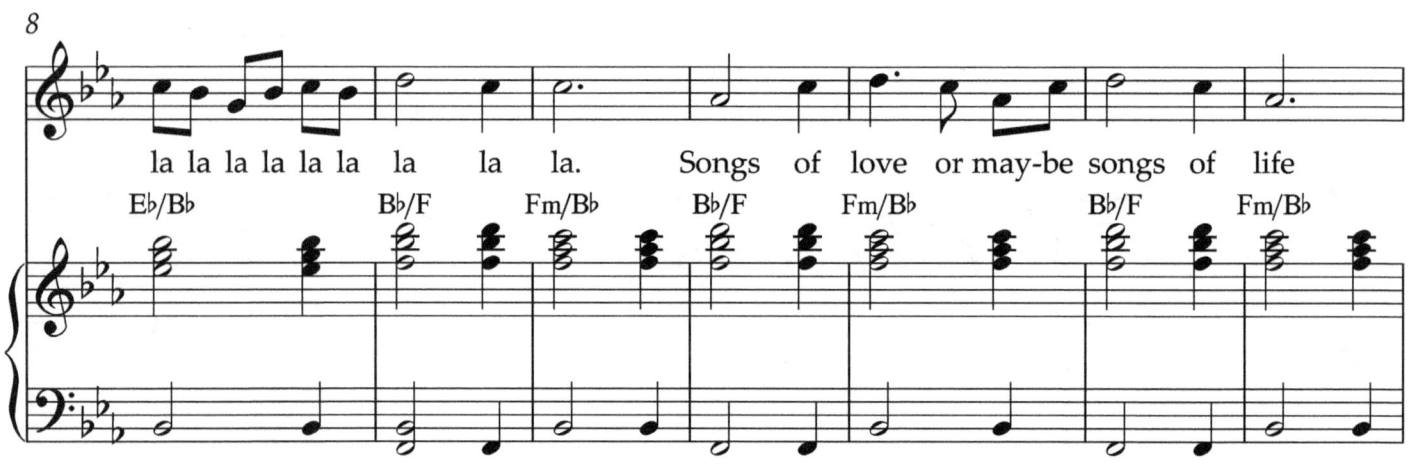

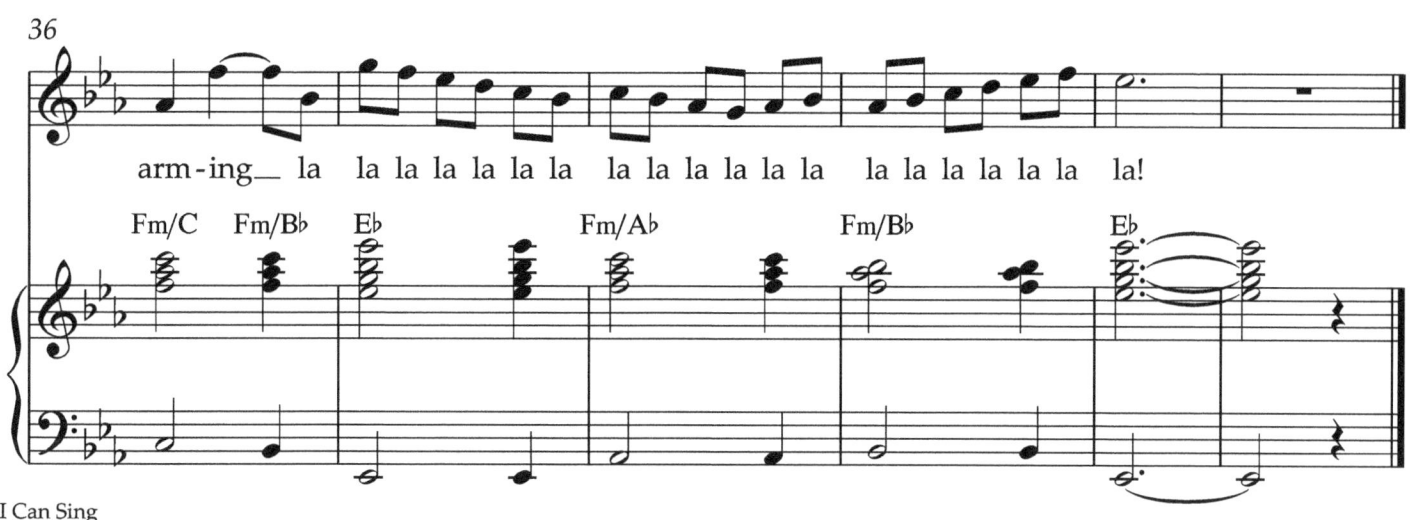

I Can Sing

Best Buddy 2nd Reprise

Words and Music by
Jan Callner

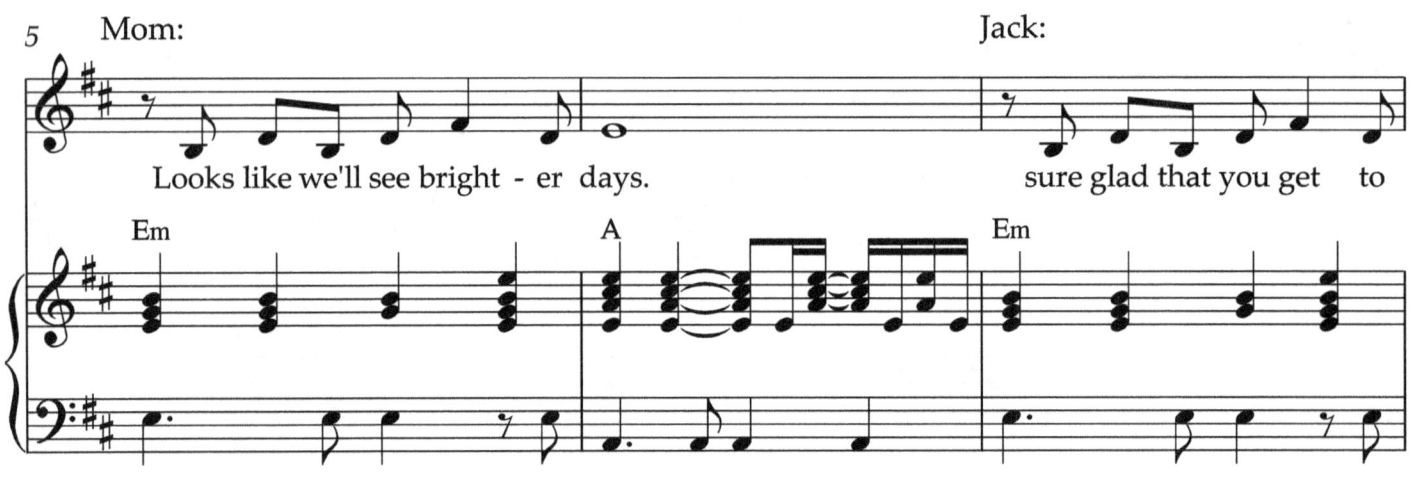

Best Buddy

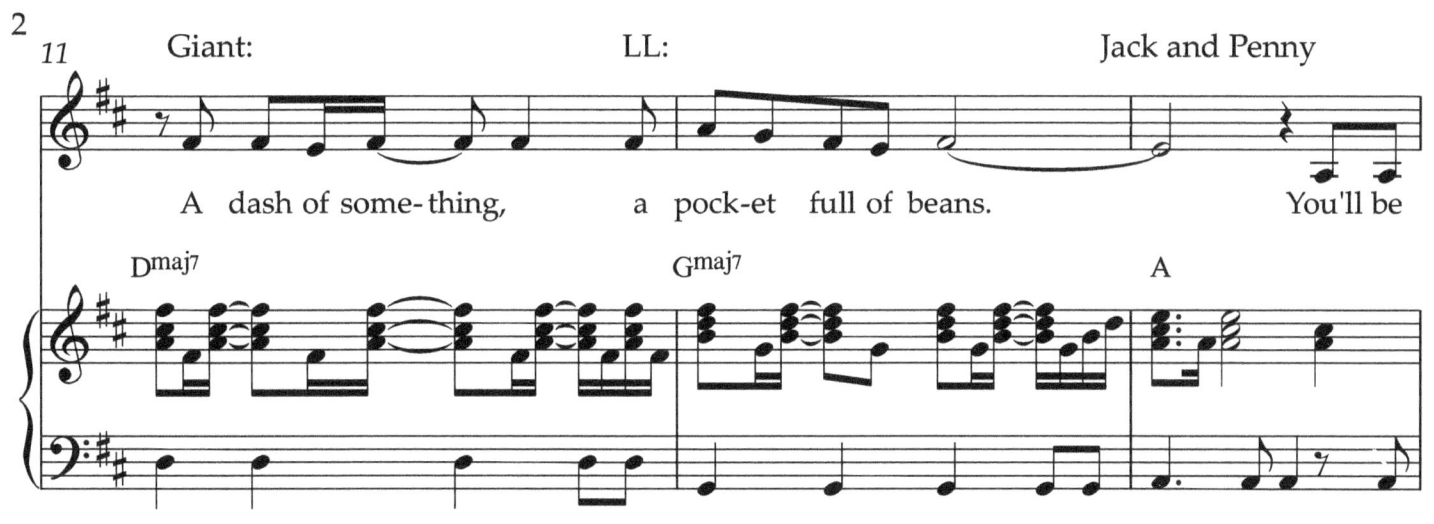

Fee Fie Foe Fum

Words and Music by
Jan Callner

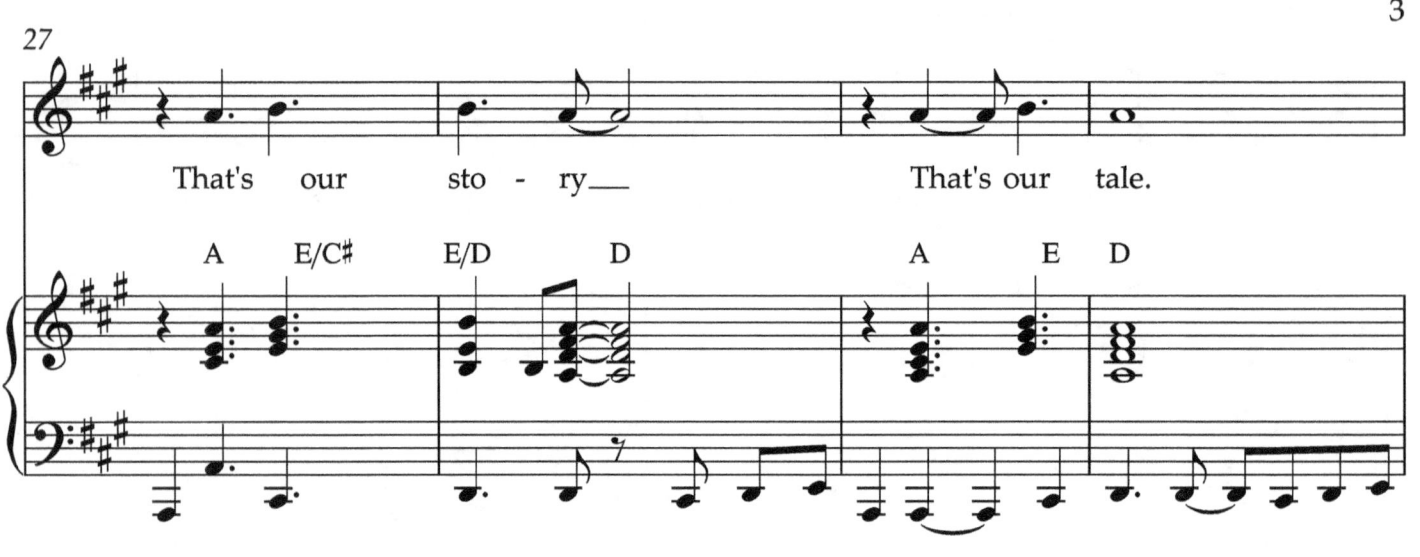
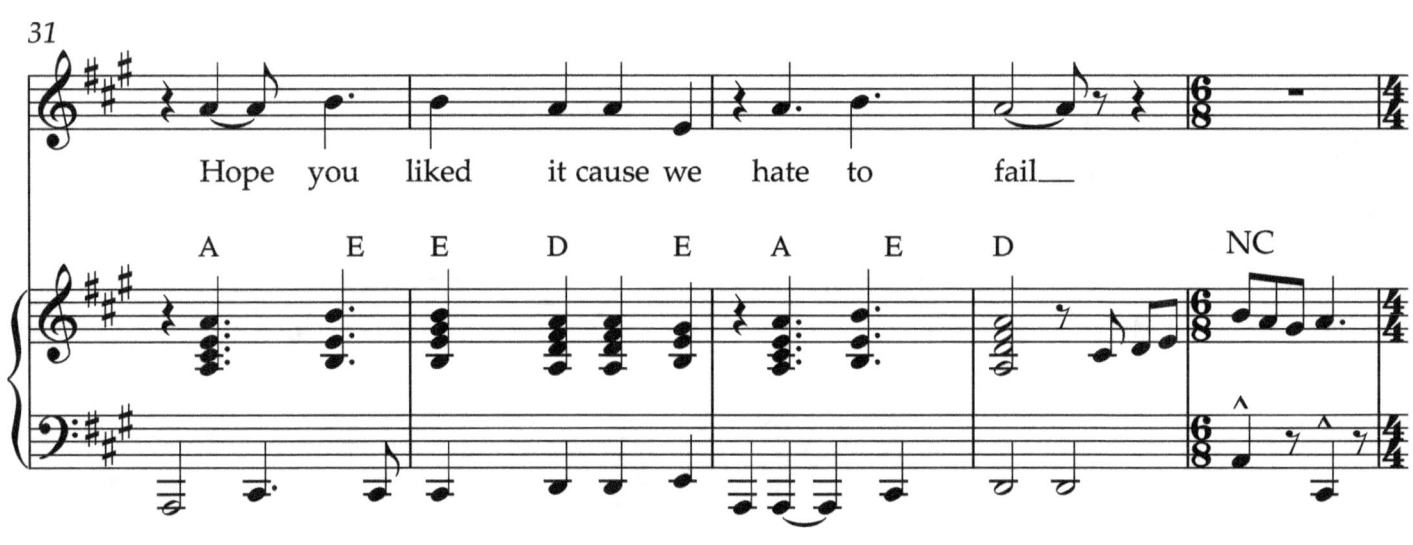

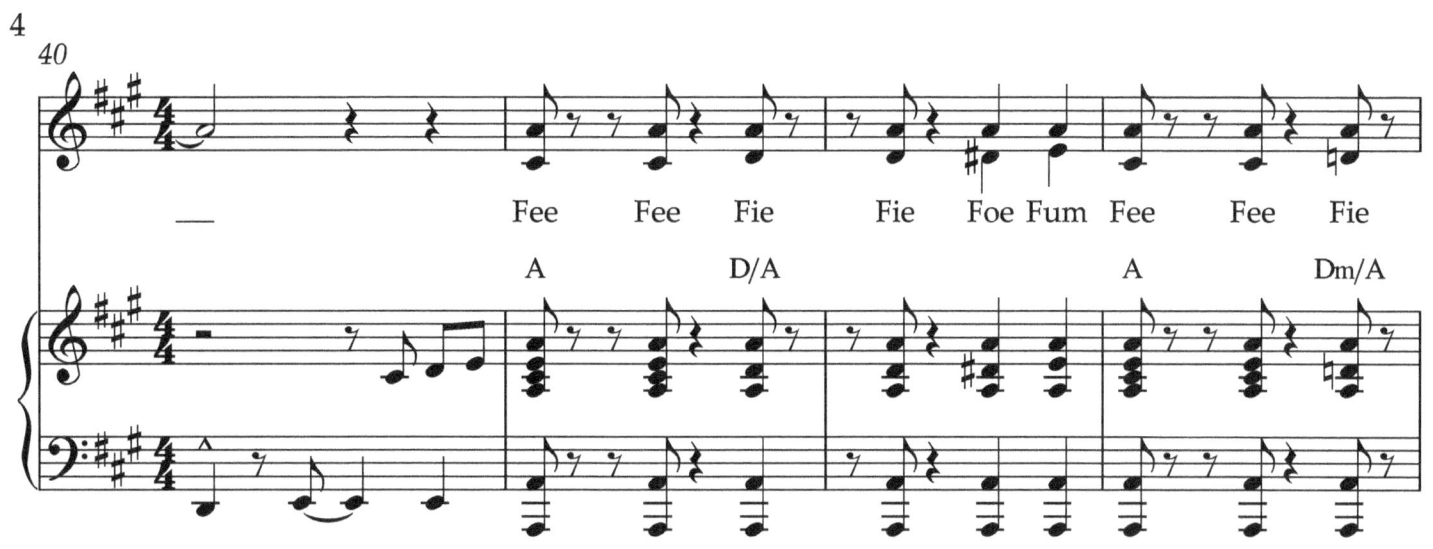
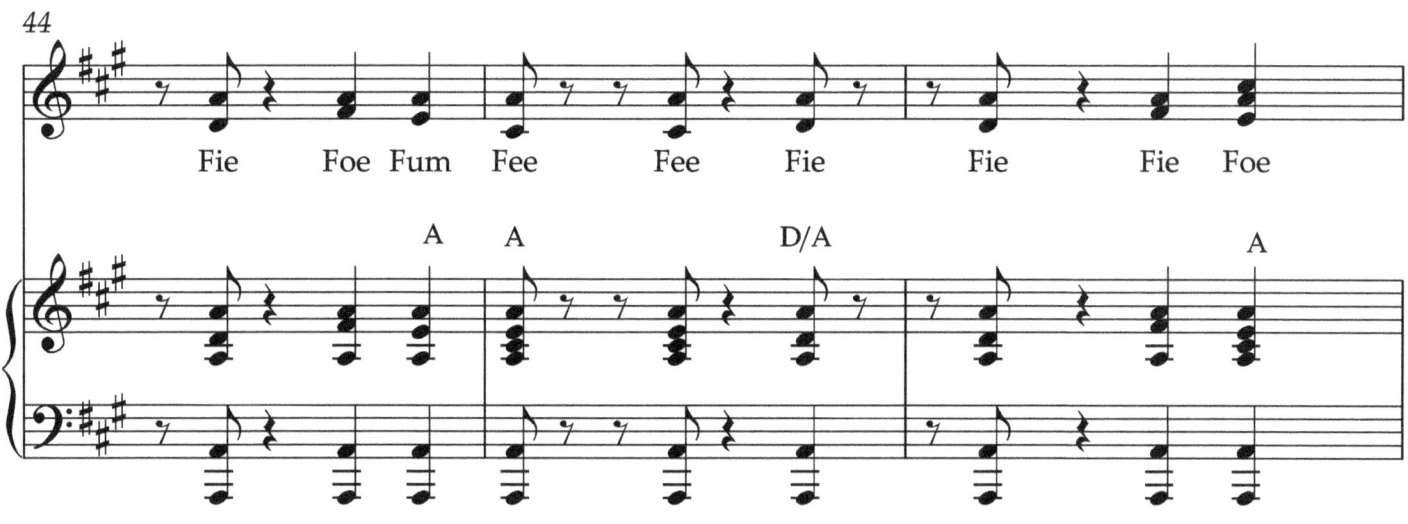
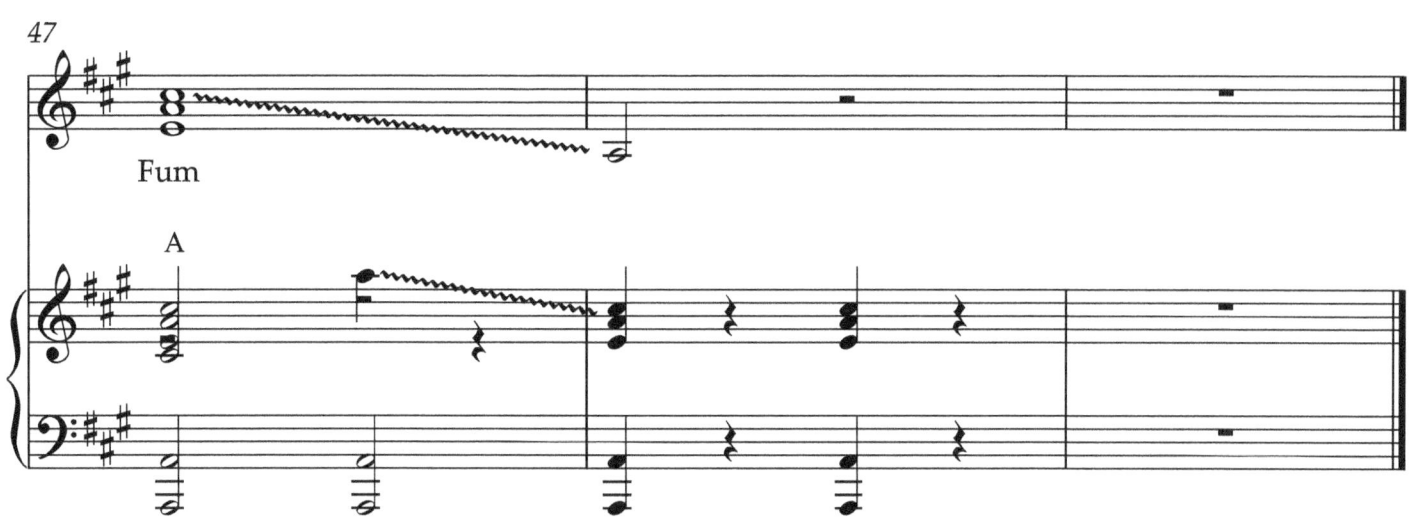